IDENTITY 2.0

YOU ARE NOT WHO YOU THINK YOU ARE

KEITH LEONARD

i·den·ti·ty

>>

/ī'den(t)ədē/

the internal characteristics determining who a person believes they are.

Copyright © 2025 by Keith Leonard
All rights reserved.

No part of this publication may be reproduced, stored in a retrieval system, or transmitted in any form or by any means—electronic, mechanical, photocopying, recording, or otherwise—without the prior written permission of the author, except in the case of brief quotations embodied in critical articles or reviews.

Identity 2.0
You are not who you think you are

First Edition
Published September 25, 2025
ISBN: 979-8-9924903-3-6
Printed in the United States of America

For permissions or bulk orders, please contact:
Inner Compass Publishing
www.InnerCompassPress.com
contact@innercompasspress.com

This book is a work of nonfiction. Some names and identifying details have been changed to protect the privacy of individuals. Any resemblance to actual persons, living or dead, is purely coincidental and unintentional.

Cover design by Inner Compass Publishing
Interior design by Inner Compass Publishing
Published by Inner Compass Publishing

IDENTITY 2.0
YOU ARE NOT WHO YOU THINK YOU ARE

Advance Praise for IDENTITY 2.0

....

"So many people who find themselves on the cusp of a career change discover that they have defined themselves solely by what they do rather than by who they are. Keith's book provides the tools to shift that dynamic and realize the freedom of instead letting your values and identity shape what you do."

— **Jennifer Y., Executive Coach with 35 years of experience leading people and complex programs.**

"There are events that changed the course of my life in the most impactful resonating way. Reading this book is one of those. Thank you, Keith, for becoming an impactful leader."

— **Pierre A. Bedard, Executive Coach**

"Identity 2.0" is a powerful, compelling, practical guide to change at the level of who you are. I believe it will help readers claim who they are becoming and act from that choice each day. I am excited for people to read it and feel that shift."

— **Valerie Galado, Head of Academic Affairs**

""What struck me most in identity 2.0 is the realization that we make a decision about who we want to be. We're constantly given the chance to align with the self that thrives. This book showed me how to choose the identity that succeeds - and everything else will follow.""

— **Robert Di Marco, Business Elevation Specialist**

....

Acknowledgements

Writing *Identity 2.0* has been one of the most meaningful journeys of my life, and I could not have done it alone.

First, I want to honor my mentor, Dr. Cloé Madanes. Your teachings shaped not only my career but also my understanding of human behavior at its deepest level. The wisdom and strategies I share in this book are deeply influenced by the foundation you created, and I am forever grateful.

To Richard Bandler and John Grinder, co-creators of NLP, and the brilliant minds who have advanced this field—Tony Robbins, Robert Dilts and Sid Jacobson—you opened the door to a way of thinking and transforming that continues to change lives, including my own.

To my colleagues and students at Robbins-Madanes Training: you inspire me daily. Your questions, breakthroughs, and commitment to growth challenged me to keep refining these ideas until they became crystal clear. This book is as much yours as it is mine.

To my clients—the executives, entrepreneurs, leaders, and dreamers I've had the privilege to coach—thank you for trusting me with your stories. Every session, every breakthrough, and every transformation reminded me of why this work matters.

To my family and friends, who have supported me with love, patience, and encouragement, even when writing consumed my energy and attention—thank you for being my anchor.

And finally, to you, the reader. Thank you for picking up this book and daring to believe that you are more than your past, more than your habits, and more than who you think you are. Without you, this book would just be words on a page. With you, it becomes a movement.

This book was written with you and for you—because the world needs the person you are about to become.

CONTENTS

Introduction — 01
You Are Not a Static Character

Chapter 1 — 11
The Identity Trap: Why Your Life Feels Stuck

Chapter 2 — 29
Understanding the Architecture of Change

Chapter 3 — 47
The Environment Lie

Chapter 4 — 65
Behavior Without Identity is Theater

Chapter 5 — 79
The Prison of "I'm Just Not Good At That"

Chapter 6 — 93
The Invisible Rules That Shape You

Chapter 7 — 109
The Identity Operating System

Chapter 8 — 123
Purpose and Spiritual Congruence

Chapter 9 — 137
Living as Identity 2.0

Chapter 10 — 153
Engineering Your Identity: The Identity 2.0 Roadmap

Final Thoughts — 225

Personal Note from the Author — 234

Bibliography & Reading Guide — 240

IDENTITY 2.0
YOU ARE NOT WHO YOU THINK YOU ARE

> "We are not what happened to us, we are what we wish to become."
>
> -Carl Jung

INTRODUCTION

"You can't outperform your identity. You will always act in alignment with who you believe you are."

— *James Clear*

Change Can Happen at Any Age

Let's start with the truth that most people forget far too early in life: it is never too late to change. Not just on the surface — but at the level that matters most. You can change how you think. You can change how you show up. You can change who you believe yourself to be. No matter how long you've lived one way, a new way is always possible. But the world rarely tells you that. Instead, it teaches you that real transformation belongs to the young — that once you've chosen a path, built a life, made mistakes, or become known for a certain way of being, that's it. You're locked in. You are who you are. Maybe you can tweak a few habits or soften a few edges, but deep change? The kind that turns your life inside out and upside down? That gets quietly filed away under "too late" or "not realistic."

And yet, here you are. Holding a book not about surface-level fixes, but about deep, identity-level transformation. Something in you already knows what the world tries to suppress — that you are still capable of becoming someone new. Someone truer. Someone more aligned. And not in a way that denies your past, but in a way that honors it without being defined by it. You are not frozen in place. You are not trapped in your timeline. You are not the sum of your age, your resume, your relationship history, or your regrets. You are a living system. And like any living thing, you are meant to evolve.

If no one has told you this yet: you are not too late. You are not too broken. You are right on time. You haven't missed your moment. This *is* your moment. And you don't need to start over — you just need to stop outsourcing your identity to the version of you that was built for survival instead of growth. You are not a static character in a story someone else wrote. You are the author. And your next chapter starts the moment you realize that identity isn't something you discover — it's something you *decide*. Right now, in this season, in this body, with this history. You don't need to go back in time. You just need to *go forward on purpose.*

My Story: The Pattern Behind Every Success and Every Setback

Looking back over the different seasons of my life — the wins, the losses, the leaps, the stalls — a clear pattern eventually revealed itself. Every time I succeeded in a meaningful way, whether in business, leadership, public speaking, or relationships, it wasn't just because I worked harder or got lucky. It was because, consciously or unconsciously, I had already started to become the kind of person who *could* succeed in that area. Before the outcome changed, the identity had shifted. I showed up differently. I spoke differently. I made decisions from a place of clarity instead of fear. I wasn't pretending or posturing — I was aligned. The success didn't just happen to me. It flowed through a version of me that I had grown into.

And the failures? They followed the same pattern — just in reverse. In the moments I stumbled, plateaued, or sabotaged myself, I was still living from an outdated version of who I thought I was. I'd shrink back into the identity of someone who felt like an imposter, or who believed he had to be perfect to be worthy, or who secretly thought, *"This probably won't work for me."*

On the surface, I was taking action. But underneath, my identity was quietly steering me toward familiar outcomes — not because I wasn't capable of more, but because I wasn't convinced I *was* more. And I see now, with uncomfortable clarity, that those setbacks weren't just about strategy or timing. They were about alignment. My external life could only stretch as far as my internal self-concept allowed.

Every time I succeeded, I had become the kind of person who succeeds. Every time I failed, I had shrunk into the kind of person who expects failure. The shift didn't begin with habits. It began with who I believed I was.

And once I saw that pattern in my own life, I started seeing it everywhere. In the people I coached. In leaders I admired. In friends who couldn't figure out why they kept hitting the same emotional wall. Behind every result — good or bad — was a belief about identity. Not always loud or obvious, but always present. And that realization changed everything. It reframed my own struggles. It rewrote my understanding of transformation. And most importantly, it gave me a path to help others who were stuck — not because they weren't trying, but because they were trying from the wrong starting point.

This is where I invite you to pause and look at your own journey. Not with judgment, but with gentle curiosity. What version of yourself were you living from when things flowed, when life opened up, when it felt easy to be brave? And what version were you in when things fell apart, or stayed small, or never quite took off? We often obsess over behaviors, tools, and tactics — but behavior is the echo of identity. It follows, not leads. If you want lasting change, you don't start with what to *do*. You start with who you're willing to *become*.

And once you understand that — really understand it — you'll never approach your life the same way again.

How This Book Works: A Map for Identity Change

This book isn't a collection of motivational stories or feel-good advice. It's a guided journey — a step-by-step path for changing your life by changing the one thing that shapes everything else: your identity. But don't worry, this isn't going to be technical or overwhelming. You don't need a background in psychology or personal development to follow what's coming. You just need an open mind, a willingness to reflect, and a readiness to tell yourself the truth. What you'll find in the pages ahead is a simple, powerful structure that makes the invisible parts of your identity visible — so you can work with them, not against them.

We'll begin with your outer world — the environment you live in, the people you spend time with, the spaces that surround you. Because even though change begins on the inside, the conditions around you either reinforce or resist that change. Then, we'll move inward, layer by layer, through your behaviors, your capabilities, your beliefs, your core identity, and finally, your sense of purpose — the deepest layer, the one that gives everything else meaning. You'll start to see how every level of your life is connected. How the clutter in your home links to the voice in your head.

How the habits you struggle to maintain are tied to the way you see yourself. How your purpose isn't something you find, but something you remember — once you peel back the layers that buried it.

Each chapter is designed to help you audit, adjust, and align. You'll find examples that feel like they were written about your own life. You'll explore questions you've never thought to ask. And you'll walk away with more than clarity — you'll walk away with language. With structure. With a way to name and navigate the parts of yourself that were never really explained to you before. And when we get to Chapter 10, you'll pull it all together into a living, breathing roadmap. That chapter is where insight becomes action — a practical toolkit filled with templates, reflection prompts, and a repeatable framework you can use for the rest of your life. Whether you're reinventing your career, healing from a setback, stepping into leadership, or simply tired of feeling stuck in a version of yourself that no longer fits — that final chapter will help you move forward with clarity and precision.

Because this book isn't just about insight. It's about engineering. You'll come away with a clear, repeatable framework for becoming who you were always meant to be.

Read With a Curious Mind

This is not a book to rush through. It's not something to check off your list or power through in a weekend. This is a mirror. A flashlight. A conversation. Read it that way. Read it with a curious mind and an open heart. Let it be personal. Let it interrupt you. Let it slow you down. If a sentence hits you, stop and sit with it. If a story feels too familiar, pause and ask yourself why. Write in the margins. Underline what stings. Reread what stirs something. Not everything here will land the same way for everyone — and it's not meant to. This isn't about agreement. It's about *inquiry*. The kind that helps you meet yourself with more honesty than you've allowed before.

If something challenges you, good. That's where growth starts — not in the comfortable truths, but in the ones you almost skipped past. You don't have to take everything at face value. Be skeptical. Ask questions. Turn the ideas over in your mind. But don't use skepticism as a shield. Use it as a scalpel. Not to cut the work down, but to cut deeper into your own understanding. Because the goal here isn't universal truth. It's *personal revelation*. The question isn't, "Is this true for everyone?" The question is, *"Where is this true for me?"* That's the question that changes everything. That's the question that puts you back in the center of your own story — not as a passive character, but as the author and architect.

This book will meet you where you are — but it won't let you stay there. It will challenge you, stretch you, and ask more of you. And in return, it will give you the tools to change not just what you do, but who you become. Read slowly. Read bravely. Read as if your future depends on it.

Because in a very real way — it does.

Expect Success

The fact that you're holding this book — the fact that something inside you was curious enough, open enough, brave enough to turn these pages — tells me everything I need to know about you. You're ready. Maybe not in every way. Maybe not all at once. But something in you has already decided that the life you're living now isn't the end of the story. And that matters more than you know.

Change doesn't begin with certainty. It begins with willingness. You've already crossed that threshold. You're not here by accident. You're here because some part of you is done waiting. Done performing. Done staying small just to feel safe. And that part of you — the one reaching forward — is the part we're going to strengthen, nurture, and build upon with every chapter from here.

As you begin this journey, remember: you are not broken. You are *becoming*. What you've called "stuck" or "lost" may have only been misalignment — living from a version of yourself that's too small for the vision life is calling you into. And as you upgrade that identity, your behavior, your decisions, your opportunities — everything — will follow.

That's not wishful thinking. That's how you're wired. By the time you finish this book, you won't just understand identity — you'll know how to *shape it, live it, and evolve it*. Not just once, but as many times as life demands it.

So take a breath.

Turn the page.

And step into the story you've always wanted to write — not by force, but by design.

Believe in the person you're becoming.

"The chains of habit are too light to be felt until they are too heavy to be broken."

-Warren Buffett

CHAPTER 1

The Identity Trap: Why Your Life Feels Stuck

You're not broken — you're misaligned. The invisible cage is your outdated identity.

You've Been Acting from an Old Script

You might not say it out loud, but something inside you knows: this life you've built doesn't quite fit anymore. On the surface, everything seems fine. You're responsible. People count on you. You handle what needs to be handled. And yet, beneath the rhythm of your daily responsibilities, there's a quiet question that keeps rising: *Is this really me?*

It's not that things are falling apart. It's more subtle than that — a persistent sense of restlessness or a low-grade discontent that you can't quite name. You wouldn't call it a crisis. You may not even think of it as a problem. But it's there. And it doesn't go away. That's because the version of you running your life — the role you've been playing — was built for a different time. It was created during a chapter that's already over. And now, you're outgrowing it.

The truth is, we all inherit roles early in life. We become "the responsible one," "the achiever," "the caretaker," or "the one who doesn't need anything." These identities are usually shaped by necessity — a response to family dynamics, cultural expectations, or the simple desire to feel safe and accepted. They worked for us once. They helped us adapt, connect, survive. But what once protected you can eventually begin to confine you.

Over time, these roles stop feeling like choices and start feeling like facts. You build your career around them. You shape your relationships to fit them. And eventually, you forget that they were ever optional. You just become that person. Until one day, something inside you realizes: *I can't grow any further as long as I keep playing this part.*

The Fatigue of Staying the Same

There's a kind of exhaustion that doesn't come from doing too much — it comes from living out of alignment. From saying yes when you mean no. From downplaying your needs, biting your tongue, or showing up in ways that no longer reflect who you are becoming. And the longer you live that way, the more it drains you. Not in the dramatic way burnout hits, but in quiet, persistent ways: procrastination, numbness, disinterest, low-level frustration. Like driving with the brakes on.

What you're experiencing isn't a failure of willpower or character. It's the friction between the life you're leading and the identity you've outgrown. And vacations, podcasts, and to-do lists won't resolve that kind of fatigue. Because this isn't about your calendar. It's about your *identity*.

We're taught to solve life's problems by working harder or being more efficient. But when the real issue is that you're living from a self-image that no longer fits, no amount of productivity will fix it. At best, it will keep you too busy to notice how misaligned you feel. At worst, it will wear you down so gradually that you forget what it felt like to feel fully alive.

Behavior Follows Identity — Always

If you've ever tried to make a change — lose weight, speak up more, be less anxious, go after a dream — you've probably noticed how hard it is to sustain. You might make progress for a while, but eventually, things drift back to baseline. You start to feel like someone who can *start* change, but not *sustain* it. And that cycle begins to chip away at your confidence.

But the problem isn't your discipline. It's not your attention span. It's not your lack of motivation. The problem is that you're trying to create next-level results without shifting the self-image beneath your actions. You're trying to act like someone you don't yet believe you are.

This is the trap no one talks about: you can set a new goal, build a new habit, or even change your external circumstances — but if your core identity remains the same, your unconscious will pull you back into alignment with who you believe yourself to be. Not who you *want* to be. Who you *believe* you are.

If you see yourself as someone who's "always overlooked," no amount of achievement will fully register. If you see yourself as someone who's "not a leader," then even when you're given influence, it will feel accidental. If you think of yourself as "just getting by," then thriving will feel like a betrayal of your story — and you'll sabotage it before it can take root.

This is why so many people stay stuck, even when they're intelligent, capable, and trying hard. Because they're working from the wrong level. They're trying to change the symptoms, not the source.

You Don't Need a New Life — You Need a New Identity

This book isn't about fixing you. Because you're not broken. It's not about motivating you with clichés or pushing you to hustle harder. You've probably already done plenty of that. This book is about something deeper — and far more powerful. It's about helping you realize that the version of you you've been living from... is just that: *a version*. A role. A script. One that you may never have consciously chosen.

And now, you get to choose.

You're not here to become someone entirely new. You're here to become more *you* — the version of yourself that's been waiting beneath the noise, beneath the performance, beneath the outdated self-image you've worn like armor.

The process of stepping into that version isn't about dramatic reinvention. It's about quiet alignment. It's about rewiring your identity from the inside out — so that your thoughts, behaviors, habits, and goals stop feeling like battles... and start feeling like truth.

In the next chapter, I'll introduce you to a powerful framework for making this shift — a way of understanding change that will make everything you've struggled with finally make sense. But for now, here's what I want you to know:

If you feel stuck, it's not because you're behind.
If you feel restless, it's not because you're ungrateful.
And if you feel like you're meant for more, it's not a delusion — it's a signal.

You're not who you think you are.
You're who you *learned* to be.

And now, it's time to remember who you're capable of becoming.

The Performance of "You"

We all play roles. Some are obvious, like the ones we slip into at work or with family. Others are more subtle — so deeply ingrained that we forget they were ever a choice. We become the responsible one, the fixer, the peacekeeper, the overachiever, the one who never asks for help. These roles are not accidental. They were shaped over time, through the expectations of others, the circumstances we lived through, and the rewards we received for acting a certain way. They made us feel safe, accepted, or valued — and so we kept playing them.

But here's the truth most people never pause to consider: *the role you've been playing is not your identity — it's a performance you learned to deliver*.

That performance likely served you once. It helped you navigate your world. It gave you a sense of control. But over time, the role that once protected you can become a prison. You find yourself over-functioning in relationships, over-committing at work, staying quiet to keep the peace, saying yes when you mean no — all to maintain a version of yourself that others expect, and that you've come to expect of yourself.

When we perform a role long enough, it fuses with our self-concept. We no longer ask, *"Is this who I want to be?"* We simply assume, *"This is who I am."* But under the surface, something doesn't feel right. You begin to feel disconnected — not from your life, but from yourself. You're showing up, doing the things, checking the boxes. But it feels hollow. Like you're playing a part in a story that no longer moves you.

This disconnection isn't a sign that something is wrong with you. It's a sign that you're evolving — but still acting from a version of yourself that hasn't caught up.

One of the most common struggles I see with high-functioning clients — people who seem successful on the outside — is this quiet inner conflict: *they're doing everything right, but it doesn't feel like them anymore.* They're exhausted from holding up the image, confused by the loss of motivation, unsure how to make a change without disrupting everything they've built. But what they're really wrestling with is an identity that's gone stale — a version of themselves that can no longer support the weight of who they're becoming.

This is where change gets hard. Because letting go of a familiar identity — even one that's hurting you — feels dangerous. You fear you'll lose stability. Respect. Relationships. Status. You wonder, *Who will I be without this version of myself? Will anyone still want me? Will I still recognize me?*

But the truth is, you're not erasing yourself. You're retiring a role. You're letting go of the performance so that something more honest, more alive, and more aligned can take its place.

When your identity matches your values — when your external life reflects your internal truth — you don't have to perform anymore. You don't need to fake confidence. You don't have to overcompensate. You don't need to prove anything. You simply *are*. Your choices start feeling congruent. Your energy returns. And your presence deepens — not because you're trying harder, but because you're finally being yourself.

This book is about helping you cross that bridge — from the old role you've mastered to the new identity that's ready to emerge. But first, we need to understand why surface-level change never lasts — and why identity always determines the ceiling of your transformation.

Let's explore that now.

The Problem of Surface Change

Most people try to change their lives by focusing on what they do. They change their schedule. They download habit trackers. They start going to the gym, waking up earlier, or setting goals. They might even tell themselves, *"This time, I'm really doing it."* And for a little while, it works. They see progress. They feel proud. But eventually — sometimes gradually, sometimes suddenly — the old patterns return. Motivation dips. Momentum stalls. The new habits begin to fade, and a familiar sense of disappointment creeps back in. They begin to wonder, *What's wrong with me? Why can't I stick with this?*

Nothing is wrong with them. What they're experiencing is the inevitable collapse of change that's been made at the surface level — without the deeper architecture to support it.

The truth is, you cannot permanently change your behavior without changing the identity that drives it. Behavior follows identity. Always. When the two are out of sync, identity wins. Every time.

Imagine trying to install cutting-edge software on a ten-year-old operating system. You can force it to work for a while. You can troubleshoot the bugs, patch the problems, and muscle your way through the updates. But eventually, the system will revert. Not because the new tools are broken — but because they were never fully compatible with the underlying structure.

This is how most people approach personal growth. They add strategies, routines, or habits to a self-concept that's fundamentally misaligned with those changes. They try to act like someone new while still believing they are someone old. And that creates a deep, invisible conflict — one that eventually pulls them back to the comfort of familiarity, even when that familiarity is painful.

For example, someone might build a habit of speaking up more in meetings. But if they still believe, *"I'm not really leadership material,"* then that behavior will always feel out of character — like an act they're trying to pull off. It won't feel natural. It won't feel safe. And eventually, it won't last.

Or imagine someone who's finally making time for their creative work — writing, painting, starting a side business. But if they still see themselves as "the practical one," or "the reliable provider," then that creative work will feel indulgent, even irresponsible. Not because it is — but because it doesn't align with their identity. And so they'll stop. Not because they didn't care, but because the role they've been living from doesn't make space for that version of themselves.

This is the unspoken reason why so many smart, capable people stay stuck. It's not a lack of tools or time or talent. It's an identity mismatch. They're trying to act differently without updating the story that governs who they believe they are.

We live in a culture obsessed with action. Do more. Be more productive. Set bigger goals. Push harder. But action without alignment is temporary. If you don't shift your self-concept, your unconscious mind will eventually course-correct — not toward your aspirations, but toward what feels familiar.

This is what people call "self-sabotage," but in reality, it's self-protection. Your mind is designed to keep you consistent with who you believe you are. When you step too far outside that boundary, it creates internal pressure — not because you're wrong, but because your inner system doesn't yet recognize this new behavior as belonging to you. So it brings you back.

And that's why change feels hard. It's not because growth is impossible. It's because you're trying to change outcomes without changing origin. You're rearranging symptoms, not healing the root.

The solution isn't to try harder. It's to go deeper.

Lasting transformation doesn't start with discipline. It starts with identity. Once you shift how you see yourself, your behavior begins to change almost automatically. You don't have to force it. You simply act in alignment with the version of yourself you now believe you are.

This is what it means to become the kind of person for whom the desired behavior is *natural*, not forced. When you shift your identity, success feels less like something you're chasing and more like something you're expressing.

Next, we'll begin to uncover where your current identity came from — and why so much of it was shaped by influences you didn't consciously choose. Because before you can step into a new story, you have to see the old one for what it is:

Not a truth.
Not a sentence.
Just a story.

And stories can change.

Stories We Mistake for Truth

Identity doesn't begin with conscious choice. It begins with interpretation.

Long before we could articulate what we wanted out of life, we were already forming conclusions about who we were — and who we were allowed to be. These conclusions weren't delivered as formal instructions. They were absorbed through experience. Through the patterns of praise and punishment. Through subtle signals from parents, teachers, siblings, and peers. Through the things we were told repeatedly, and the things we noticed no one ever said.

Over time, we stitched together an understanding of ourselves: *I'm the smart one. I'm the shy one. I'm the one who gets it done. I'm the one who never gets chosen. I'm the helper. I'm the disappointment. I'm the survivor.* These aren't statements we wrote down in journals. They live deeper than that — embedded in the nervous system, confirmed through repetition, rarely questioned, rarely challenged.

What most people don't realize is that these self-statements — these "I am" beliefs — are not truths. They are stories. Stories that were constructed under pressure, often before we had the capacity to interpret life accurately. And once those stories settled into place, we began living them out. Not because we were destined to, but because we believed we had to.

This is the invisible mechanism behind much of human behavior: *the need to stay consistent with the story we've accepted as "me."* Once you believe something about yourself — especially if that belief formed under stress or pain — your mind begins to collect evidence to support it. Not out of malice, but out of loyalty. The brain craves certainty. And the most certain thing it knows is your identity story.

So if your early experience taught you that speaking up gets you punished or ignored, you learn to shrink. If you were rewarded for being accommodating, you learn to equate worth with self-sacrifice. If you were constantly compared to others, you learn to define yourself by what you lack. These patterns become internal law: *Don't take up space. Stay in control. Never need too much. Be impressive, or be invisible.*

And you carry those laws into adulthood — into your work, your relationships, your goals, and your habits — often without realizing you're still obeying them.

The problem isn't that these stories exist. The problem is that we forget they're stories.

We confuse them with facts. We say things like *"I've always been this way"* or *"That's just not me."* But these aren't objective realities. They're narratives that became reinforced through emotion and repetition — often in moments where we didn't feel safe, seen, or free to be ourselves.

And if you never revisit those stories, they quietly become your ceiling. They shape what you believe is possible, what you tolerate, what you pursue, and what you leave behind. They define the limits of your self-permission.

The tragedy is not that these stories were formed. The tragedy is that we let them harden into identity. That we live out scripts written by fear, scarcity, or survival — long after we've outgrown the need for them.

But here's the good news: if your identity was shaped by stories... then it can be reshaped by better ones.

This doesn't mean rewriting history. It means rewriting your relationship with it. It means becoming aware of the assumptions you're still living by — and choosing whether they deserve to remain part of your story.

You might realize that what you called "being responsible" was actually a child learning to carry too much. That what you called "not being creative" was really a teacher's offhand comment that shut something inside you down. That what you called "not being leadership material" was just a pattern of self-doubt built from trying to earn approval you never needed to earn in the first place.

None of this awareness is about blame. It's about reclamation. Because once you see your identity as a narrative — not a fixed reality — you regain authorship. You stop being the actor in someone else's script. You become the writer of your own.

Before we conclude this chapter, let's look at what happens when those old stories begin to break down — when the role you've been playing becomes too small for who you're becoming.

We'll look at what most people call a crisis… and reframe it for what it really is: an invitation.

Because if you've started to feel like something inside you no longer fits, you're not falling apart. You're growing.

And the discomfort you feel isn't confusion. It's clarity — asking to be heard.

The Identity Crisis as an Invitation

There comes a point — often quietly, sometimes suddenly — when the life you've built begins to feel misaligned. It's not always dramatic. You may still be doing well by external standards. You're showing up, fulfilling your roles, checking the boxes. But something inside you is shifting. You begin to feel disconnected from your own success, restless in your own routines. The life you created no longer feels like it reflects who you are. Or more accurately, who you're becoming.

What most people call a breakdown is often something far more profound: the moment when your old identity begins to loosen its grip.

This isn't something to fear. It's something to notice.

You're not broken. You're being invited.

We usually think of identity crises as problems to solve or avoid. They feel uncomfortable, inconvenient, even threatening. And it's no wonder — the structures we once relied on for a sense of self begin to wobble. The roles, routines, relationships, and rules we've lived by start to lose clarity. Things that used to make sense no longer do. Goals that once excited you now feel empty. The version of yourself that once fit so well now feels like a costume that's grown too tight.

But what if that discomfort isn't a sign that something's wrong? What if it's a sign that something inside you is ready to grow?

An identity crisis, if you allow it, can become one of the most powerful turning points in your life. It is the moment when autopilot breaks down, and conscious authorship begins. It's when the old story starts to feel foreign — not because you've failed, but because you've evolved. The beliefs and behaviors that once kept you safe now keep you small. And life, in its own wise way, refuses to let you shrink any further.

What makes identity transitions so destabilizing is that they feel like loss. And in some ways, they are. You're grieving an older version of yourself — one that carried you through hard times, that earned praise, that helped you belong. But you're also outgrowing it. And growth always costs comfort.

There's fear here, of course. Fear of letting go without knowing what comes next. Fear of disappointing others. Fear of becoming someone unrecognizable. But beneath all that fear is something else — something even stronger: *a pull toward truth*. A desire to finally live in alignment. To stop performing. To stop striving.

To stop trying to earn a sense of worth that should have never been in question.

This is not the collapse of your identity. It's the emergence of a new one — one that's built not from habit or history, but from choice. From values. From vision. From clarity.

The discomfort you feel? That's not confusion. That's the friction between who you've been and who you're ready to become.

This book is your guide through that transition.

You don't need another list of things to do. You need a new way to *be*. A new way to see yourself — one that's big enough, honest enough, and flexible enough to contain your future. You're not here to become someone else. You're here to become someone more *you* than you've ever allowed yourself to be.

In the next chapter, we'll begin to look at the structure of change — the architecture beneath every transformation, from surface habits to the deepest layers of self-concept. You'll learn why most personal growth strategies don't stick, and why real, sustainable change must begin at the identity level.

But for now, here's what I want you to hear:

If you've been feeling off, you're not failing — you're waking up.

If you've outgrown your current life, it's not the end — it's a beginning.

And if you've been questioning who you really are, it

means you're finally close enough to the truth to feel it.

This is not a breakdown... It's an invitation.

And it's time to answer it.

> "You can't change what you don't understand."
>
> —Toni Morrison

CHAPTER 2

Understanding the Architecture of Change

Real change is multi-layered. Your identity sits atop a pyramid you've likely never examined.

What If Change Has a Structure?

Most people approach change as if it's a matter of effort. Try harder. Focus more. Get disciplined. Make better choices. We tend to think that if we could just *do* the right things consistently, we'd become the person we want to be. And when that approach doesn't work — when the habits fade, the motivation dips, and the old patterns creep back in — we blame ourselves. We assume we weren't committed enough. That we lack willpower. That we're just not the kind of person who can change.

But what if the problem isn't your effort — what if it's your approach?

Imagine trying to fix a cracked foundation by painting the walls. It might look better for a little while, but the underlying problem hasn't been resolved. Eventually, the cracks reappear — maybe in new places, maybe deeper than before. That's what most self-improvement strategies do. They try to fix surface issues without addressing the deeper structures that created them.

The truth is, change is not one-dimensional. It doesn't happen in a straight line, and it doesn't begin at the surface. Real, sustainable transformation isn't just about what you do. It's about what drives what you do. It's about what you believe, what you expect, how you see yourself, and what role you think you're here to play in the world.

You've probably noticed this in your own life. You've made changes before — maybe you changed your diet, your routine, your job, or your relationships. And for a while, things improved. But then, almost without noticing, you slipped back into something familiar. The new behavior didn't stick. The new results didn't last. Not because you failed — but because you hadn't changed the layers of yourself that made the old behavior feel natural.

It's not that change isn't possible. It's that change made from the wrong level is rarely permanent. If you want to change your outcomes, you have to work from the inside out — from the deeper architecture of who you are and how you've been conditioned to show up in the world.

This inner structure isn't visible. You won't see it in your calendar or in your checklist. But it exists. And if you don't understand it, you'll continue trying to rearrange the furniture in a house that's sinking into the ground.

True change — the kind that lasts — begins by understanding how these deeper layers influence your decisions, your emotions, your actions, and your identity. Not just what you're doing wrong, but *why you keep doing it*. Not just what you want to become, but *what's in the way of becoming it.*

Most people never realize this. They keep trying to solve the problem they can see, instead of understanding the problem that's shaping it from beneath the surface.

But once you do see it — once you understand the underlying structure of personal change — everything else begins to make sense. The failed attempts, the repeated patterns, the internal resistance... they all become understandable. And more importantly, *they become changeable.*

Let's begin to uncover what this inner structure looks like — and how your current sense of self may be built on layers you've never fully examined.

Because the solution isn't to force yourself into change.

The solution is to *understand yourself more deeply than you ever have before* — and rebuild from there.

The Pyramid Beneath Your Identity

If you've ever felt like you were changing and not changing at the same time, you're not imagining things. You were likely making progress on the surface while being quietly anchored to something deeper. This is one of the most overlooked truths about personal growth: you are not just one thing. You are a layered system. And unless you know which layer is creating the problem, you'll keep trying to fix your life from the wrong place.

Think of yourself like a multi-story building. The ground floor is your external world — where you live, who you're around, what your daily environment looks like. Above that are your actions — the things you do, the routines you follow, the habits you repeat. The next floor up is your skillset — what you know how to do, the strengths you've developed. Above that is a room filled with beliefs — the rules you live by, many of which you didn't consciously choose. Then comes your self-image — the way you define who you are and what you're worth. And at the very top, there's something even more powerful: your sense of purpose. Why you believe you're here. What it all means.

This model of layered change draws heavily on the work of Robert Dilts, who expanded on Gregory Bateson's original "Logical Levels" framework — a map for understanding the different layers of human experience and how shifts at one level ripple through the rest.

Each of these layers influences the ones below it. When the upper floors shift, the lower ones follow. But if the lower levels change without adjusting the foundation above, the structure becomes unstable. It wobbles. It collapses. And when it does, most people go right back to their old patterns — not because they want to, but because they've been trying to grow in a way that doesn't align with who they believe they are.

You can rearrange your environment. You can upgrade your habits. You can even learn new skills. But if the beliefs, identity, or sense of purpose driving those changes don't shift, you'll eventually sabotage your progress — or quietly resent it.

This is why change so often feels frustrating. Because you might be making bold moves on the outside while dragging around outdated programming on the inside. You're trying to act like someone who wants more, but you're still running the internal narrative of someone who doesn't believe they're allowed to have it.

Let's make this real.

You might start setting boundaries in your relationships, but if you still believe you have to earn love by being accommodating, those boundaries will feel selfish — and you'll abandon them the first time someone pushes back.

You might practice public speaking, network more, or start putting yourself out there at work. But if your identity still says, *"I'm not someone people take seriously,"* then every one of those efforts will feel like a performance — something to endure rather than something to own.

Or you might change jobs, move to a new city, or pursue a new goal. But if you haven't updated the internal story that tells you what kind of life you're allowed to have, you'll find a way to recreate the very discomfort you were trying to leave behind.

This is not self-sabotage. This is self-consistency.

Your mind is constantly working to keep you in alignment with who you believe you are. Not who you say you want to be. Not who other people think you are. But who you *expect* yourself to be, at the deepest level.

The key to lasting change is learning to identify which layer of your internal structure is generating resistance — and working at that level, rather than blindly repeating surface-level efforts. For some, the sticking point is external — they need to change their space, their relationships, or their routine. But for most people, the real work lives higher up the structure: in their beliefs, their identity, and their purpose.

Those are the levels where transformation becomes sustainable. That's where behavior change becomes effortless. That's where alignment happens — and from alignment, momentum becomes natural.

In the rest of this chapter, we'll explore why most personal development strategies focus only on the lower layers — and why that's not your fault. You'll also discover where the true leverage point lives — and how your identity has been quietly shaping every part of your life, often without your permission.

But before we go there, just sit with this idea:

You're not failing because you haven't changed. You're stuck because you've changed at the wrong level.

Once you find the right one, everything begins to shift.

Why Most Self-Help Fails (And Why It's Not Your Fault)

If you've ever read a self-help book, joined a challenge, downloaded a planner, or started a new morning routine only to find yourself circling back to the same stuck place weeks later... you're not alone. And more importantly, you're not broken. You were just working with the wrong blueprint.

Most self-help approaches are well-intentioned. They offer tools, tips, and inspiration. They tell you how to improve your time management, eliminate distractions, speak with more confidence, or think more positively. And often, these strategies *do* work — for a while. You get a burst of progress. You feel the high of momentum. You start to believe, *"Maybe this is it."*

But then — slowly or suddenly — something shifts. You get busy. You get distracted. You get discouraged. The old patterns return, like muscle memory. And just like that, you find yourself right back where you started. Only this time, it feels worse. Because now there's not just frustration — there's shame. *"Why can't I stay consistent? Why do I always end up here?"*

That shame is undeserved.

Because the truth is, most self-help strategies target the part of you that's easiest to reach — your behavior — without addressing the part of you that holds the most power: your identity. And when your actions aren't supported by a new internal self-concept, the change will always collapse under its own weight.

Here's the problem: behavior is what people see, so it's what gets the attention. It's what can be measured, tracked, and celebrated. But behavior is also the *most fragile* part of transformation. It's the final output, not the origin. It's the symptom, not the root. And when you try to change the symptom without healing the source, you may feel better temporarily, but you never feel *different*. You're still you — trying to live someone else's life.

This is why you can build habits and still feel hollow. It's why you can set goals and still feel lost. It's why you can reach milestones and still feel like an imposter.

Because no matter how good the system is, no matter how consistent the habits are — if they're stacked on top of an identity that hasn't changed, they will eventually be rejected.

Not because they don't work. But because they don't belong — not yet.

You don't rise to the level of your plans.
You fall to the level of your self-concept.

Let's make this tangible.

You might set a goal to double your income. You invest in the training. You learn the tools. You build the funnel or apply for the promotion. But if you still see yourself as someone who never quite measures up, who's always playing catch-up, then no matter how much money comes in, you'll find a way to feel just as scarce. You'll undercharge, overwork, or spend it faster than you earn it. Not because you're bad with money — but because your identity isn't wired for abundance yet.

You might try to improve your health. You get the gym membership. You clean up your diet. You follow the plan. But if deep down you believe you're the kind of person who "can never stick with anything," then that belief will shape your energy, your consistency, and your self-talk until the old habits come rushing back.

You might even begin to speak up more, take on leadership roles, or start your own business. But if you still carry the belief that you're not someone people listen to — that you're not naturally confident, or that you're faking it — then you'll spend more energy managing your image than expressing your power. And that disconnect will eventually lead to exhaustion or withdrawal.

This isn't self-sabotage. It's self-alignment.

Your inner world is always trying to create consistency between your identity and your experience. And when your external actions outpace your internal beliefs, your system will pull you back to what feels familiar — even if what's familiar is miserable.

This is why most self-help fades. Not because the advice is bad. But because it only reaches the surface.

If you want to make lasting change, you have to shift the inner narrative that determines what kind of person you believe you are. You have to work at the level where behavior is no longer something you *try* to maintain — it's something you *naturally express*.

This isn't about working harder. It's about working deeper.

It's about upgrading the core architecture that's been running your life — often without your awareness — and beginning to reshape it from the inside out. When that happens, your goals no longer feel like effort. They feel like integrity. They stop being things you're striving toward, and start being things you're *finally aligned with*.

Next, we'll explore the center of that architecture — the part of you that governs how you interpret success, how you respond to failure, and what you believe you're capable of.

This is the real pivot point.
It's not behavior. It's not belief.
It's the answer to the question: *Who do I think I am?*

Identity Is the Pivot Point

If there's one truth that separates fleeting change from lasting transformation, it's this:

You will never consistently act in a way that contradicts who you believe you are.

You might force it for a while. You might white-knuckle your way through the new behavior. You might even convince people around you that you've changed. But if the change lives only in your behavior — and not in your *identity* — it will always feel like effort. Like a mask you're wearing, rather than a reflection of who you've become.

Identity is the pivot point. It's the inner compass that determines not just what you do, but *how you interpret what you do*. Two people can perform the exact same behavior — start a business, run a marathon, speak on stage — and experience it completely differently. One feels like they're expanding into who they are. The other feels like they're pretending, performing, waiting to be exposed.

The difference isn't talent. It's identity.

Identity answers the question most people aren't asking consciously, but are living unconsciously: *What kind of person am I?*

And here's the thing — it's not a philosophical question. It's a *patterned reality*. You live your answer every single day. In how you talk to yourself. In what you tolerate. In what you pursue and what you avoid. In how much success, love, visibility, money, joy, or rest you allow yourself to experience without guilt or sabotage.

This is where most change efforts fall apart. Because identity operates like a thermostat. It sets the temperature for what feels normal, safe, and expected in your life. You might raise the temperature for a bit — get the promotion, land the client, lose the weight, start the project — but if that new result doesn't match the temperature your identity is set to, your system will regulate it back down.

You'll find a way to mess it up, walk it back, or explain it away. Not because you're incapable of success, but because you're still internally calibrated for *less* than what you're reaching for.

This is not conscious. It's coded. And unless you deliberately choose to update that code, you will spend your life bouncing between bursts of progress and quiet regression, wondering why you can't seem to hold onto what you've worked for.

The people who create real, sustained change — the kind that feels both expansive and stable — are not just disciplined. They are *congruent*. Their actions, beliefs, and identity are working in harmony, not at odds. They're not trying to become someone else. They've become more of who they were always capable of being.

And here's the most empowering part: identity is not fixed.

You may have inherited a version of yourself from your past — shaped by your upbringing, your experiences, your environment, and your early emotional survival strategies — but you are not required to keep living from that version. You can decide to update it. Not by pretending. Not by faking confidence. But by *choosing* who you want to be... and proving it to yourself one decision at a time.

Identity is not something you discover. It's something you *design*. You don't find your true self by thinking about it — you create it by living in alignment with your values, your vision, and your truth.

You begin to act as the person you want to become. You start to gather evidence that you *are* that person. And then one day, something subtle but profound happens: you stop trying to change. You simply *are* changed.

Your behavior is no longer in conflict with your identity. It's an expression of it.

This is the point where growth accelerates. Because when your internal story says, *"This is who I am,"* and your external behavior matches that story, you feel powerful. You feel clear. You feel like you're moving through life with alignment instead of resistance.

Everything gets easier — not because life becomes less challenging, but because *you're no longer in your own way.*

In the next section, we'll bring this into focus even further. You'll begin to understand how all the different layers of your life — your routines, your skills, your beliefs, your purpose — are shaped by the identity you've been carrying... and how to start using that layered structure not just as a theory, but as a map.

A map to rebuild your life from the inside out.

Using the Levels as a Map

By now, you've probably started to sense it: change isn't random. It's not just a matter of doing more or trying harder. It has a shape. A structure. An internal sequence. And when you work with that structure — instead of fighting against it — change becomes less about discipline and more about alignment.

The challenge is that most people have never been taught to see their inner world this way. They've been handed techniques, rules, and routines — but no map. No way to understand which part of themselves is actually creating the resistance they keep running into. So they try to change everything at once, or they obsess over surface-level fixes, or they chase yet another system that promises clarity... but delivers only temporary momentum.

Without a map, even your best efforts will feel scattered. You'll take action in one area of life, but feel like you're being pulled backward in another. You'll start to make progress, but then hit the invisible ceiling of your beliefs. You'll upgrade your habits, but still feel unworthy of the results. And eventually, it will seem easier to settle than to fight a battle you don't understand.

But what if you had a way to see exactly where the misalignment lives?

What if you could trace your frustration — not to a flaw in your character — but to a mismatch in the layers of your identity?

What if you could look at any area of your life and ask, *Where's the real friction? Is it my environment? My behavior? My skills? My beliefs? My sense of self? Or my lack of deeper purpose?* — and then know exactly where to intervene?

This is what the next chapters will give you.

We're going to walk through each layer of your internal architecture — from the outer world you operate in, all the way to the inner truth you live from — and rebuild each one, deliberately, in alignment with the person you're becoming.

You'll start by looking at your environment: not just where you live, but what you tolerate. The people you surround yourself with. The spaces you occupy. The stimuli you allow into your system every day. Most people underestimate how deeply their physical and social environments reinforce their current identity — and how much they'll need to shift in order to create space for the new one.

Then we'll move into behavior: the choices you make, the actions you repeat, and how to ensure they're not just "productive" — but identity-aligned. You'll learn how to stop trying to become someone else and instead start *acting like yourself on purpose*.

From there, we'll examine your capabilities — the skills you've built and, more importantly, the ones you've avoided building because of an outdated belief that says you're not "that kind of person." We'll deconstruct that myth and show you how developing new capabilities isn't just practical — it's symbolic. Every new skill you build is a vote for the person you're becoming.

We'll then go deeper — into the territory of belief. The internal rules you've been living by. The limits you've accepted as truth. And we'll begin rewriting those stories, not by blind optimism, but by consciously choosing what you want to believe — and backing those beliefs with action, evidence, and alignment.

And from there, we arrive at the center: identity. The source code. The hidden script. You'll explore the self-image you've been living from — most of which was formed without your conscious consent — and begin constructing a new version of yourself based not on fear, approval, or adaptation... but on *choice*.

Finally, we'll elevate to the highest level of all — the one most people skip entirely: purpose. Not a vague slogan or a perfect plan, but a meaningful orientation to your life. A sense of direction that gives your growth context and your identity gravity. Because when you're clear on why you're here — even if that purpose evolves — the rest of your system begins to organize around that clarity.

This is not about changing everything at once. It's about changing what matters most — in the order that actually works.

As we move forward, you'll begin to see your entire life differently. Not as a set of disconnected problems to fix... but as a system to realign. A pattern to update. A structure to rebuild — from the inside out.

You don't need to be perfect. You just need to be intentional.

You don't need to become someone else. You just need to stop living as a version of yourself that no longer fits. And you don't need to do it all today. You just need to take the next honest step — starting with the most overlooked force shaping your life: *Your environment.*

"Until you make the unconscious conscious, it will direct your life, and you will call it fate."

-Carl Jung

"You are a product of your environment. So, choose the environment that will best develop you."

-W. Clement Stone

CHAPTER 3

The Environmental Lie

You've believed your surroundings define you – but you can curate your environment for transformation.

You Are Not Your Circumstances

We tend to think of our environment as something we live in — a backdrop, a setting, a collection of people, places, and obligations we've either chosen or inherited. But most of us rarely consider how much influence that environment has on our behavior... and more importantly, on our identity.

Your environment is not just where you are. It's who you're being trained to stay.

The spaces you inhabit, the people you interact with, the conversations you overhear, the notifications you receive, the expectations placed on you — all of these are shaping you in real time. Not dramatically. Not loudly. But subtly. Gradually. Persistently. They're reinforcing the version of you that you're used to being. And unless you pause to examine that influence, it becomes almost impossible to separate who you truly are from what you've been unconsciously conditioned to become.

Most people don't realize this. They think they're making free choices, acting independently, living on their own terms. But their patterns — their moods, their ambitions, their self-perception — are being quietly calibrated by the environment they're embedded in. It's like being inside a room with a thermostat set five degrees too low. You'll always be a little colder than you want to be, and you'll start to believe that's just the way things are. Eventually, you stop reaching for the dial.

You learn to adapt. You learn to tolerate. You learn to shrink.

Think about the places you spend the most time — your home, your workplace, your digital landscape. Do those environments reflect the version of you you're becoming? Or do they silently pull you back into the version of you you're trying to outgrow?

If your workspace is chaotic, cluttered, and reactive, it's not just unproductive — it's programming you to stay scattered, overwhelmed, and always behind.

If your home is filled with reminders of who you used to be — objects from a life you no longer feel connected to, obligations you no longer want to carry — it's not just nostalgic. It's anchoring you to a self-image that no longer fits.

If your social circle constantly reinforces old narratives — the "you" who was always the helper, the one who never speaks up, the one who plays small to keep the peace — then you're not just dealing with people. You're dealing with mirrors that refuse to reflect your growth.

Your environment is a living feedback loop. It's either reinforcing your current identity or supporting your next one. And the longer you live inside an environment that contradicts your transformation, the harder that transformation becomes.

This is why so many people feel stuck — even when they're motivated, even when they've done the inner work. Because their outer world is out of sync with their inner evolution.

They're trying to become someone new while staying surrounded by everything that was built for the old version of themselves.

They keep returning to old routines, old triggers, old roles — not because they're addicted to suffering, but because they haven't changed the physical, relational, and digital spaces that keep pulling them back.

Here's the truth most people miss: If you want to become someone new, your environment has to evolve with you.

You don't have to burn everything down. But you *do* have to become intentional.

You have to ask: *What in my current world reinforces the version of me I no longer want to be?* And *what would my environment look like if it was designed to support who I'm becoming?*

This is not just about optimizing your surroundings. It's about *taking your life off autopilot* — and realizing that your environment has been writing your script for far too long.

It's time to take the pen back.

Up next, we'll examine how the people closest to you — often unconsciously — reinforce the very identity you're trying to move beyond. Not because they mean to hold you back, but because they're responding to the version of you they've always known.

And if you want to grow into someone new, you'll have to learn how to navigate something most people avoid:

Outgrowing the roles that keep your relationships comfortable — but keep you small.

The People Who Keep You Small

One of the most powerful forces shaping your identity isn't internal — it's social. The people closest to you often have the strongest opinions about who you are, and without realizing it, they reflect that image back to you in subtle, persistent ways.

That reflection may be comforting. It may even be loving. But it is not always aligned with your growth.

We are relational beings. We develop our sense of self by how others respond to us. In childhood, that dynamic is necessary — our identity forms through attachment, feedback, approval, and modeling. But what starts as development can become entrapment. Because once people get used to a certain version of you, they rarely want that version to change. Not because they want to harm you — but because *your identity supports theirs*.

You were the reliable one. The easygoing one. The fixer. The achiever. The one who didn't ask for much. The one who kept the peace. And the longer you lived in that role, the more other people began to rely on it — even expect it. Your predictability became their stability. And any attempt to shift that role, even for your own growth, will be felt as a disruption in the system.

This is why change — especially identity-level change — often triggers resistance not just from within you, but from the people around you.

You start saying no where you used to say yes. You start speaking up where you used to stay quiet.

You start taking risks, slowing down, setting boundaries, or prioritizing yourself.

And suddenly, things feel... off.

People question you. Tease you. Distance themselves. Not always harshly — often with a smile or a joke. *"You're not really like that." "You've changed." "Don't be so serious."* They're not rejecting you — they're reacting to the discomfort of your transformation.

We like to think of relationships as stable, but they're actually built on *roles*. And when one person stops playing their part, the entire system wobbles. That wobble doesn't always mean the relationship will break — but it does mean the relationship must *reorganize* around a new version of you.

Some people will adjust. Some won't. And that's the emotional cost of growth that few are willing to name: if you evolve, not all of your relationships will come with you.

That's not a failure. That's reality.

And it doesn't mean you need to cut people out of your life in some dramatic fashion. But it *does* mean you need to become aware of how your social environment is either supporting your next chapter... or silently keeping you in the last one.

Are you being reflected back to yourself in a way that expands your sense of possibility?

Or are you being cast in a role you've outgrown?

Are you surrounded by people who see your potential and challenge your limits?

Or by people who are more comfortable with your past than your future?

This is not about blaming others. It's about reclaiming your authorship.

You don't need everyone to understand your growth. You don't need permission to become someone new. But you *do* need to stop outsourcing your self-image to people who are invested in the old you.

As you shift your identity, your relationships will enter a phase of recalibration.

Some will get stronger — because they're based on connection, not control.

Some will get quieter — not out of malice, but because growth reveals differences that were always there.

And a few may fall away — not because you failed them, but because the relationship depended on you staying small.

That's the hidden cost of transformation: *you may have to grieve the comfort of who you used to be — and the comfort others found in that version of you.*

But what you gain is far greater: integrity, clarity, and relationships built around who you really are, not who you've been performing to be.

Now, we'll explore another layer of your environment — one that shapes your identity constantly, often without your awareness: the spaces you occupy and the stimuli you allow in.

Because it's not just people that shape your self-image. It's *everything around you*.

Your Space Is a Feedback Loop

Your environment doesn't just surround you. It speaks to you. It teaches you how to feel, how to think, how to move through the day. Whether you're aware of it or not, your space is constantly sending messages — and those messages reinforce the version of yourself you're used to being.

Every object, every layout, every sound and screen is part of a loop: you shape your space, and your space shapes you.

Consider your morning. Before you even make a conscious decision, your environment has already nudged you toward certain behaviors. Maybe your phone is the first thing you touch. That screen pulls you into a world of other people's priorities before you've even remembered your own. Maybe the lighting in your bedroom is dim, the air is stale, the clutter is visible before your feet hit the floor. Your body registers all of this — even if your mind doesn't. You're already being cued to feel behind, scattered, or low-energy... and the day hasn't even started.

None of this is accidental. It's patterned. And patterns — repeated over time — shape identity.

When you walk into a space that reflects the past, your mind behaves like it's still living in it. The piles of paper on the counter. The projects left unfinished. The items tied to an older version of your goals, your relationships, your lifestyle. These aren't just things. They're stories. Every time you see them, even briefly, they whisper a message: *This is who you are.*

And if you're not careful, you start believing it.

Your external environment is an extension of your internal one. Clutter is rarely just a mess — it's a mirror. A reflection of decisions unmade, boundaries unspoken, dreams deferred. It's the visible result of tolerations — the things you've been putting up with for so long, you've stopped noticing how heavy they've become.

And it's not just about physical clutter. Digital environments matter too. The apps you check. The inbox you dread. The endless scroll of content that fills the gaps in your day. All of it is part of your identity system. You consume what's familiar. You click what you've clicked before. You follow people who reflect a version of life you've either settled into... or feel secretly ashamed for not having.

These signals accumulate. Not in one loud moment, but over days, weeks, years. Until one day, you forget that your environment is changeable — and you begin to see it as *inevitable*.

But it isn't.

You are not your space. You are not your inbox. You are not the room you woke up in, the office you sit in, or the feed you scroll through.

But if you don't intervene — if you don't interrupt the loop — your space will quietly keep you locked into the life you've already outgrown.

Here's the shift: you must begin to see your environment not as a reflection of your past, but as a tool for shaping your future.

What would it look like if your physical space was designed to reinforce the identity you're stepping into?

What if your home wasn't just a place to sleep, but a sanctuary that reminded you — daily — of your worth?

What if your desk wasn't a dumping ground for tasks and tension, but a command center for creativity and clarity?

What if the digital world you scroll through wasn't feeding you fear, comparison, or distraction — but vision, truth, and alignment?

Changing your space isn't about aesthetics. It's about *identity engineering*. It's about replacing friction with flow. Noise with clarity. Dead weight with momentum.

When your environment becomes a reflection of who you are *becoming*, your habits stop feeling like effort. They feel obvious. Aligned. Natural.

This is why even small changes can have a powerful impact. Cleaning a space. Letting go of objects that belong to a former version of you. Creating visual cues that reinforce who you now choose to be. These are not superficial upgrades. They are declarations.

Declarations that say: *I'm not waiting for change. I'm preparing for it.*

So, now let's talk about how to do that with intention — how to become the architect of your environment, instead of its prisoner.

Because your space can either reinforce your old story...

Or it can help you rehearse your new one.

Changing the Stage, Not Just the Lines

Imagine trying to deliver a powerful new performance... while standing on the same old stage, under the same dim lighting, surrounded by the same cast of characters who only know your last role. It doesn't matter how much you've rehearsed your new lines — if the stage hasn't changed, the audience (and your nervous system) will expect the same act as before.

That's what most people are doing when they try to change their lives without changing their environment. They're reciting a new script — but in a setting that only recognizes the old version of them. No wonder it feels like the transformation doesn't stick.

If you want to embody a new identity, you can't just act differently. You have to *build a world* that supports that difference. You have to *design the stage* so your new role feels natural, not forced.

Most people underestimate how powerfully our surroundings cue our behavior. We think our actions come from willpower or discipline. But more often, they come from cues. Subtle signals. Triggers. Patterns baked into the places we inhabit. Walk into a kitchen, and you might feel the urge to snack — not because you're hungry, but because your body recognizes the context. Sit at your desk, and your posture, attention span, even mood may shift — not because of what you're working on, but because of what that desk represents.

So if you want to shift behavior, you don't just need motivation. You need *context engineering*.

Changing the stage means asking yourself a different set of questions:

- *What visual cues in my environment reinforce the old version of me?*
- *What spaces make me feel small, distracted, or stuck?*
- *Where do I feel most aligned, most present, most powerful — and why?*
- *What elements of my space could be redesigned to match the identity I'm building?*

Sometimes, the changes are obvious. Clear the clutter. Remove the distractions. Rearrange the room. Change the lighting. Display a symbol or object that represents the person you are becoming.

Other times, the shifts are more symbolic — but just as powerful. Removing items that anchor you to an outdated story. Changing the artwork that evokes a feeling of nostalgia or loss. Rearranging the furniture so that you *feel* like you've moved forward, even if you haven't left the room.

These aren't superficial moves. They are physical affirmations.

You are telling your nervous system: *we live differently now.*

And it responds.

Your digital environment deserves the same attention. Curate your inputs. Unfollow the accounts that keep you tethered to comparison, fear, or distraction. Mute the noise. Rearrange your phone so that inspiration is easier to access than anxiety. Turn your browser into a portal for your vision, not a trapdoor into someone else's.

Even the language you use with yourself — your internal environment — needs a redesign. Do you speak to yourself like someone becoming more? Or do you use the same old scripts of guilt, doubt, and delay?

Changing the stage means reimagining your entire world — physical, digital, relational, internal — as a place designed for expansion.

Because when the stage supports the role, the performance becomes easier. When your environment reflects your evolution, your actions begin to align. And when you stop trying to change while everything around you stays the same, you finally give yourself the leverage you've been missing.

In the next and final part of this chapter, we'll give you the tools to take action — to become the architect of your world, not just the actor in someone else's.

Because identity doesn't just emerge from the inside out. It also grows from the outside in.

And the more intentional your environment becomes, the more natural your transformation will feel.

Becoming the Architect of Your World

At some point, you realize that waiting for your life to support your growth is a losing game. The people, places, and routines that shaped who you've been won't automatically evolve to match who you're becoming. That shift — the one that makes real change sustainable — only begins when you stop reacting to your environment and start *designing it*.

You become the architect.

This doesn't mean you have to move across the country, buy new furniture, or start deleting every contact in your phone. It means you start making your space — and your daily surroundings — a conscious reflection of your chosen identity, rather than a container for your unconscious past.

That shift in mindset is where real power begins.

Because once you see yourself as the architect, you stop settling for surroundings that sabotage your growth. You stop tolerating rooms that deplete you. You stop justifying clutter that anchors you to confusion. You stop making excuses for relationships that keep you walking in circles. And you start to realize something quietly revolutionary:

You don't have to feel different to start behaving differently.

You have to behave differently *in an environment that supports it*.

Designing your environment isn't about chasing perfection. It's about creating friction *against* regression — and flow *toward* your future.

Want to wake up earlier? Make your bedroom a sanctuary, not a cave. Leave your journal on the pillow. Put your phone in another room. Place a glass of water by your bed. Your identity begins before your alarm goes off.

Want to eat better? Clear the pantry. Put what you want to consume at eye level. Set the table like someone who honors their health. Don't rely on willpower to overcome convenience — change the convenience.

Want to be more focused and creative? Design a workspace that speaks to your clarity. Close the loops — visual, emotional, digital. Make inspiration easy to access and distraction harder to reach.

Want to feel more confident? Wear the clothes that align with how you want to feel — even if no one sees you. Upgrade your lighting. Adjust your posture. Let your mirror reflect not just your face, but your future.

Want to step into your next chapter? Walk through your current one like it's your proving ground. Set micro-environments — your car, your phone, your living room — as allies to your intention, not anchors to your past.

These aren't aesthetic improvements. They are structural interventions. They are reminders that say, over and over again: *You've already started becoming*.

You are not just changing your environment.

You are signaling to yourself that you deserve a life that matches your intention. You are aligning your surroundings with your identity. You are removing the friction that keeps you small and building a stage for your next act.

And most importantly, you're creating a world where the behaviors of Identity 2.0 feel obvious, natural, even inevitable.

Because when your environment supports your expansion, change no longer feels like a battle. It feels like the next logical step.

In the next chapter, we'll explore why trying to act differently — without tying those actions to a new identity — often leads to failure, burnout, or feeling like a fraud.

Because behavior change is not enough.

Not unless you know how to *turn it into evidence* for who you are becoming.

"Your environment will eat your goals for breakfast if they aren't aligned with your identity."

-James Clear

"People act in accordance with who they believe they are, not who they want to become."

-Dr. Robert Cialdini

CHAPTER 4

Behavior Without Identity is Theater

Acting different doesn't make you different – unless you attach those actions to identity.

Why Habits Fail (And How to Make Them Identity-Based)

We've been taught to believe that success is built on behavior. If you want to change your life, you need better habits. More discipline. Clearer goals. And to a point, that's true — behavior is the visible part of change. It's where momentum lives. It's what you can measure, track, and check off. But here's what most people miss: behavior is never just about behavior. It's an expression of identity.

And if your actions aren't aligned with your self-image, no amount of effort will make them stick.

That's why people can commit to a new habit for a few weeks — waking up early, eating clean, journaling, saying no, showing up more boldly — and then, one day, the behavior collapses. Not because they're lazy. Not because they didn't want it. But because deep down, it never felt like *who they are*. The habit required constant willpower because their identity never agreed to it.

When you try to behave like someone you don't believe you are, the brain interprets that behavior as temporary. A phase. A performance. And your unconscious, always aiming to preserve your self-concept, will quietly pull you back to what's familiar — even if what's familiar is painful.

This is why you've probably felt that invisible pull back to "normal" after a burst of motivation. You did everything right: made the plan, started strong, even saw some early results. But then... resistance. Self-doubt. Distraction. Life happened. And before you knew it, you were back in the same groove, frustrated with yourself for "falling off."

But you didn't fall off. You *reverted*. And you reverted not because of failure — but because your actions were ahead of your identity.

That's why the key to lasting change isn't just repetition — it's *reinforcement*.

Every time you take a new action, your brain asks, *"Is this me?"* And if the answer is no, the behavior stays fragile — vulnerable to stress, fatigue, and even success. But if the answer becomes yes — if your identity starts to absorb the behavior — that action becomes part of your operating system.

You don't just *do* the new thing. You become the kind of person who does it.

That shift — from behavior to identity — is what turns habits into transformation.

You don't just write every morning. You become a writer.

You don't just work out. You become someone who honors their body.

You don't just speak up. You become someone who owns their voice.

You don't just say no. You become someone who respects their time and energy.

This is the deeper game. And most people never learn to play it.

They keep trying to act their way into a new life... without realizing they're still being the same person underneath. They try to change their behavior without changing the story that behavior lives inside of.

They say things like "I'm trying to be more disciplined," or "I'm not really a morning person, but I'm working on it," or "I know I'm not confident, but I'm forcing myself to speak up more." And every one of those statements, while well-intended, reinforces the old identity. It's behavior as theater. You're playing the role, but you haven't yet rewritten the character.

So the behavior eventually crumbles — not because you weren't good enough, but because it was never fully *yours*.

Here's the truth: identity-based change doesn't mean pretending. It means acting in alignment with who you *choose* to become — and collecting evidence, day by day, that this version of you is real.

This is how change becomes sustainable. You take an action. You notice the action. You link that action to your new identity. And you do it again — not just for the habit, but for the *evidence* that you're becoming someone new.

Next, we'll explore the subtle moments where this reinforcement happens — what we call Mirror Moments — and how to use them as powerful tools for building your Identity 2.0.

Because change isn't something you perform.

It's something you *embody*.

Mirror Moments

The most powerful shifts in your identity don't happen during grand gestures or life-altering events. They happen in small, quiet moments that seem meaningless to everyone else—but you feel them. These are the seconds in your day where you stand at a crossroads, even if just for a breath, and you sense the difference between who you've been and who you're trying to become. These are *Mirror Moments*—the brief, ordinary choices that, over time, define who you believe yourself to be.

Maybe it's the moment you get home from a long day and instinctively reach for your phone to scroll. But something inside you pauses—*You said you wouldn't do this anymore.* You hesitate. You look at your journal on the table instead. That's a mirror moment. Maybe it's the moment in a conversation where you usually laugh to keep the peace, avoid conflict, or deflect with sarcasm. But this time, you stay still. You speak plainly. You let the silence sit. That's a mirror moment too.

Most people miss these. They're too subtle, too easy to justify or ignore. We tell ourselves, *It doesn't matter. It's just one time. I'll do better tomorrow.* And maybe we will. But what we don't realize is that each of these moments is casting a vote. Not just for what we do—but for who we are. Every action you take in private, every time you follow through when no one is watching, every decision you make that slightly tilts you toward your next self rather than your former one—these are how identity is built.

Your brain remembers patterns. It collects evidence. It builds stories around what's familiar and safe. If your daily choices reinforce the old story—*I always give in, I never follow through, I just can't help myself*—then that story becomes reinforced as fact, even if it's fiction. But when your behaviors begin to disrupt that pattern—*I got up when I said I would, I chose the hard thing over the easy one, I didn't abandon myself again*—your brain takes note. And the story begins to shift.

This is why discipline and motivation often fall flat. We treat them like tools, but they're really side effects—natural byproducts of an identity that feels real and earned. When your actions line up with the person you believe yourself to be, doing the right thing stops feeling like effort and starts feeling like alignment. You're not fighting your way forward anymore. You're following through because that's who you are now.

Mirror moments don't require perfection. They require presence. You won't win every time—and that's not the point. The point is to *notice* when you're at the fork in the road. To slow down just long enough to ask yourself: *Which version of me am I feeding right now?* Because whichever self you feed—through the smallest behaviors, the quietest choices—that's the one that grows.

And the more mirror moments you consciously move through, the easier it becomes to trust your own evolution. Not because you've arrived, but because you've seen yourself choose differently—even when it would've been easier not to. And that's where belief in the new you begins to solidify: not in declarations, but in decisions. Not in what you promise, but in what you *practice*.

The "Pretend Until You Become" Principle

There's a popular phrase in self-help circles: *"Fake it till you make it."* For some, it feels inspiring. For others, it sounds hollow—like putting on a mask and hoping no one notices you're drowning underneath. But when you look beneath the cliché, there's a deeper psychological truth worth reclaiming. The path to becoming someone new almost always begins by acting in alignment with the version of you that doesn't fully feel real *yet*. And that's not faking—it's rehearsal.

When a stage actor steps into a role for the first time, they don't believe they *are* the character. They're exploring. Trying on the posture, the tone, the choices. And with each repetition, their nervous system adjusts. Their voice stops wavering. Their movements become fluid. Their decisions seem natural. At a certain point, the lines blur—they're no longer pretending. They've become.

The same process applies to identity. If you wait to feel confident before speaking boldly, you may never speak at all. If you wait to feel worthy before setting boundaries, you'll keep giving yourself away. If you wait to feel like "the kind of person who works out," you'll stay on the couch convincing yourself that motivation will show up someday. It won't. Not reliably. But you can act in ways that make confidence, worthiness, and motivation *easier to believe in*.

Pretending isn't being inauthentic. It's expanding your emotional and behavioral range until your system catches up with your vision. Pretending interrupts the old narrative that says *this is who I am*...

and replacing it with small, repeatable acts that suggest, *Maybe I'm becoming someone else.*

Here's the paradox: you don't become someone new by waiting to feel different. You become someone new by behaving differently, consistently, until that behavior becomes part of your identity. You don't have to believe the whole story right away. You just have to act out one line of it, again and again, until the story begins to believe you back.

That means showing up to the gym not as someone who's "trying to get fit," but as someone who already values their health—even if the mirror hasn't caught up yet. It means speaking your truth not as someone "working on being assertive," but as someone who respects themselves enough to be honest. It means walking into the room like you belong there—even when your heart is racing—because the new version of you *does* belong there.

The brain is a pattern-recognition machine. It watches what you do and updates its internal model accordingly. If you keep showing up as a person who follows through, who leads, who takes care of their body, who speaks clearly, who honors their values—eventually, it stops feeling like an act. It starts feeling like the truth. The real you isn't the past you. It's the one you're rehearsing into existence.

So no, you're not faking it. You're *training* for it. You're practicing the identity you want to own until it no longer feels like a stretch. And when it stops feeling like a stretch, that's when the change sticks—not because you forced it, but because you *proved it.*

Repetition and Evidence

Identity doesn't change because you have a breakthrough. It changes because you collect *evidence*—and that evidence builds through repetition. Most people treat personal transformation like a lightning strike: sudden, dramatic, life-altering. But real change is more like a slow burn. It gathers momentum through small, repeated actions that gradually shift the story you believe about yourself. If you want to build a new identity, you have to give your brain proof that it's safe to believe in something new.

This is why consistency matters more than intensity. A single bold action feels good, but it's not enough to move the identity needle on its own. It has to be followed by another, and another, until your nervous system stops interpreting the behavior as a threat and starts accepting it as part of the norm. Think of it like forging a new path through a forest. The first time you walk it, you're pushing through resistance. Branches hit you in the face. The trail is unclear. But if you keep walking it—day after day—it starts to clear. The old path grows over. And soon, the new way becomes the default route.

Your brain operates the same way. It's always looking for patterns it can automate. So if you repeatedly act in alignment with your emerging identity—even in small ways—your mind begins to treat that behavior as who you are, not just what you're doing. And once your identity accepts a new behavior as part of "what we do," you no longer have to wrestle with it. The resistance fades. The friction drops. It becomes *obvious*.

This is why people who seem highly disciplined are often just highly aligned. They've done the work of linking their behaviors to their sense of self. They don't ask, *Should I do this today?* They just do it—because it's who they are. It's not heroic. It's rehearsed. And it's rehearsed enough times that they've gathered sufficient evidence to believe it's real.

The problem is that most people don't give themselves enough credit during this phase. They wait for external validation—results, praise, recognition—before they feel allowed to own the new identity. But that's backward. External results often lag behind internal change. If you wait for your life to reward your efforts before you claim the new self, you'll be constantly second-guessing and self-abandoning. You have to gather *internal* evidence first—by paying attention to what you're actually doing differently.

Did you show up today?

That counts.

Did you follow through even though you didn't feel like it?

That counts.

Did you pause instead of reacting automatically?

That counts.

Did you take one action that reflects who you want to be—not who you've been?

That counts too.

Track it. Write it down. Reflect on it. Build a personal archive of evidence. Your brain won't believe in the new you just because you say it. It will believe because you *show it*.

Repetition without reflection becomes routine. But repetition *with* reflection becomes reinforcement. And reinforcement is what rewires identity—not in one big moment, but across hundreds of small ones, practiced in the direction of who you're choosing to become.

The Identity Feedback Loop

Change becomes sustainable when your behavior no longer feels like effort, but like *evidence*. The key to this shift lies in what I call the Identity Feedback Loop—a self-reinforcing cycle where every action you take either confirms or contradicts the story you believe about who you are. It works like this: your identity shapes your behavior, your behavior produces outcomes, and those outcomes feed back into your sense of identity. Most people live inside this loop unconsciously, which is why they stay stuck. But once you learn how to use it on purpose, it becomes one of the most powerful tools for transformation you'll ever have.

Let's take a simple example: someone who believes, "I'm not good with money." That belief subtly shapes their decisions—they avoid budgeting, spend impulsively, and ignore their bank account. Those behaviors create predictable results: overdrafts, stress, and guilt. And those outcomes reinforce the original belief: *See? I knew I wasn't good with money.* The loop closes. Identity reasserts itself. The person stays trapped not because they lack intelligence or discipline, but because they're living in a feedback loop that always delivers evidence for the story they started with.

But here's the powerful part: the loop works in *both* directions. If you interrupt the cycle—if you change the behavior even slightly—you start to create new evidence. You make one mindful financial decision. You track a small expense. You transfer five dollars to savings. That single act becomes a crack in the identity wall. You begin to think, *Maybe I'm the kind of person who takes care of money*. That new belief changes the way you behave tomorrow. You take another action that reinforces the shift. And soon, a new feedback loop begins to form—not from willpower, but from *alignment*.

This is how people who once felt lost, undisciplined, or inconsistent begin to embody a new identity. Not because they overhauled everything overnight, but because they interrupted the loop. They realized that their actions don't need to match how they *feel*—they need to match who they *want to be*. And by choosing that alignment repeatedly, they created a new set of outcomes... which reinforced the new belief... which produced even more aligned behavior. Momentum kicks in. Confidence rises. The loop spins forward.

The mistake most people make is trying to change everything at once, expecting the new identity to emerge fully formed. But identity is forged, not flipped. It's constructed moment by moment, through actions you repeat and reflections you internalize. The more you see yourself doing what your future self would do, the easier it becomes to believe that version of you is already here.

This is why it's not just about action—it's about *meaning-making*. If you go to the gym but think, *I'm just forcing myself to do this*, you reinforce the belief that you're not someone who belongs there. But if you reframe it—*This is what someone who values their health does, and I'm becoming that person*—you strengthen the loop in your favor. The same action, two different stories. One keeps you stuck. The other moves you forward.

Your brain is listening to how you interpret your own life. It's waiting for cues about who you are. So give it clear, consistent signals. Take the action. Notice the action. Attach meaning to the action. Then repeat. That's the loop. And the more you live inside it deliberately, the faster your identity shifts from theory into truth.

In the next chapter, we'll go deeper—into the world of skill and capability. Because many of the limits we place on ourselves—*I'm just not good at that, I've never been that type of person, I can't learn that*—aren't about ability at all. They're about identity confusion. And it's time to clear that up.

> "Every artist was first an amateur."
>
> -Ralph Waldo Emerson

CHAPTER 5

Capabilities, Skills, and the Prison of "I'm Just Not Good At That"

You are not your limitations. You are your training—or lack of it.

You're Not "Bad at That" — You're Untrained

It's easy to believe that ability is personal. That some people are just "naturally good" at things, while the rest of us are left fumbling in frustration. But that belief — as common as it is — isn't just wrong. It's dangerous. Because once you decide you're not good at something, you stop trying. You stop exploring. You stop allowing yourself to grow. And just like that, your identity shrinks to fit the story you've told yourself.

Think about the last time you said something like, *I'm not creative,* or *I'm terrible with numbers,* or *I've never been good at speaking in front of people.* Were you making an observation — or were you making a decision? Most people don't realize how early these identity labels are formed. Maybe you struggled with math in school, and a teacher — frustrated or flippant — told you you just weren't wired that way. Maybe you froze during a class presentation and felt the sting of embarrassment, so you quietly vowed never to put yourself in that position again. Maybe your art or writing didn't get the praise you hoped for, so you assumed you must not be talented. Over time, these little moments calcify into "truth." Not because they are true — but because you stopped testing them.

What we call capability is often just the result of exposure and repetition. The reason someone else makes it look easy isn't because they're better than you. It's because they've practiced — even if they didn't realize they were practicing. The confident speaker you admire has probably given hundreds of talks. The savvy entrepreneur you envy has made countless mistakes behind the scenes. The calm, grounded person in your life likely spent years learning how to regulate their emotions. What looks like natural ability is usually invisible effort.

But instead of interpreting skill gaps as invitations to grow, we turn them into identity statements. We say, *That's just not me.* And the moment you say that, you build a wall between the person you are and the person you could become. That's the prison of capability confusion: believing your current limitations are permanent rather than trainable. And the longer you stay in that prison, the more you start decorating the walls — reinforcing the narrative with every missed opportunity or excuse.

Here's the good news: you are allowed to be unskilled without being unworthy. You're allowed to be a beginner. You're allowed to try something and fail — and then try again, not because you're bad, but because you're *in training*. This isn't about delusion or ego. It's about reclaiming the power to grow. And growth requires friction. You won't feel instantly good at things you've never practiced. That's not a sign to quit. It's a sign to keep going.

You don't need to have it all figured out. You just need to stop telling yourself that your past defines your potential. You can learn anything — public speaking, leadership, boundaries, negotiation, creativity, fitness, emotional regulation, confidence — if you're willing to show up with humility and consistency. But you have to drop the story that says *I'm just not wired for this*. That story isn't your truth. It's your avoidance.

Now, let's take a closer look at how these limiting identity labels are formed — and how education, upbringing, and even praise can lock us into fixed patterns that limit our evolution. Because if you've been confusing capability with character, it's time to untangle the two.

The "Fixed Identity" Illusion

There's a moment in childhood when we stop asking who we might become and start accepting who we've been told we are. For some, that moment is subtle — a lukewarm report card, a disapproving look, a comparison to a sibling who always seemed to get it right. For others, it's loud and clear — a parent saying, *"You're not a leader,"* or a teacher deciding, *"You're not college material."* These messages, whether spoken or implied, begin to form the scaffolding of a self-image that feels less like a choice and more like a life sentence.

And so we shrink to fit it.

This is the illusion of a fixed identity — the false but persistent belief that you are a certain "type" of person with a predetermined ceiling. It's the belief that you're good at some things and bad at others, not because of exposure, practice, or passion, but because it's "just who you are." It shows up in statements like *I'm shy, I'm not a people person, I've never been good at technology, I'm not a risk-taker,* or *I could never do what she does.* These identities become so familiar that we stop questioning them. We build lives around them. We make decisions from them. We even sabotage opportunities that contradict them — because success in those areas would threaten the story we've been living in.

But here's what most people don't realize: these identity statements often begin as coping strategies. They were formed not out of truth, but out of protection. If you failed at something once and felt shame, it was safer to say, *"I'm just not good at that,"* than to risk trying again and failing harder. If your effort went unnoticed or unrewarded, it was easier to decide you didn't care than to keep pushing. Over time, these protective mechanisms harden into personality traits — not because they reflect who you truly are, but because they helped you survive.

Unfortunately, what protects us early in life often imprisons us later.

The fixed identity illusion becomes especially strong when it's reinforced by well-meaning praise. If you were labeled as "the smart one," you may have learned to avoid situations where you might struggle or look foolish. If you were "the athletic one," you may have dismissed your creative side. If you were "the responsible one," you may have learned to suppress your needs and always put others first. Praise can be just as confining as criticism when it limits the full range of who we're allowed to be.

So we grow into adults with talents we've never tested and possibilities we've never pursued, all because of a story we didn't write. We call it our "personality," but more often, it's a script. A protective, inherited, outdated script that needs to be rewritten if we're going to evolve.

The good news is this: identity is far more flexible than we've been led to believe. Neuroscience confirms that the adult brain is capable of incredible change — not just in what we know, but in how we see ourselves. But the change doesn't begin with more effort. It begins with permission. Permission to question who you think you are. Permission to set down the labels that no longer serve you. Permission to see your "weaknesses" not as flaws, but as underdeveloped areas waiting for practice and patience.

Up next, we'll dive into how learning — real, engaged, identity-expanding learning — can become a symbolic act of rebirth. Because gaining a skill isn't just about competence. It's about reclaiming agency over the person you're becoming.

Learning as a Rebirth Ritual

There is a quiet power in learning something new — not just because it adds to your skill set, but because it subtly reshapes your self-concept. To learn is to declare, *"I'm not finished."* It is an act of rebellion against the fixed identity you've been carrying, especially if that identity has told you that you're too old, too late, too far behind, or too damaged to change. Every time you deliberately learn something new — a skill, a mindset, a habit, a perspective — you're not just acquiring knowledge. You're rehearsing your rebirth.

Learning, when done intentionally, is not just educational. It's *transformational*. It interrupts the inertia of who you've been and invites you to step into someone more expansive, more capable, and more in control. You are not becoming someone else. You are simply reclaiming the parts of yourself that were dormant, discouraged, or disqualified. In this sense, learning becomes a kind of sacred ritual — a process through which you discard outdated stories and experiment with new ways of being.

But for this to happen, learning must be approached differently. Not as something you do only when required, or for the sake of achievement, but as an act of personal evolution. You're not just learning to get better at something. You're learning to become someone you've never fully allowed yourself to be. This might mean learning how to speak with confidence after years of shrinking. Or how to manage your finances when you've always believed money wasn't your thing. Or how to code, or paint, or lead a team, or set boundaries — not because the world demands it, but because a deeper part of you wants to grow.

The key is to approach this kind of learning with presence, not pressure. Too often, we bring our perfectionism and performance mindset into the learning process. We think we're supposed to master everything immediately. But growth doesn't happen in a straight line. It's messy. It's vulnerable. It requires you to be bad at something long enough to get good at it — and to not make that struggle mean something negative about who you are. In fact, it's the very act of facing that discomfort that makes the transformation meaningful.

That's why your willingness to learn — even awkwardly, even slowly — is itself an identity shift. It moves you from the static realm of "This is who I am" into the dynamic space of "This is who I'm becoming." And once you step into that space, your entire orientation toward life begins to change. You stop fearing discomfort. You start seeking it out — not as punishment, but as proof that you're alive, engaged, and in motion.

Most people don't need more talent. They need a new relationship with effort. A new story about what it means to struggle. Because when struggle is no longer interpreted as failure, it becomes fuel. When learning is no longer seen as remedial, it becomes revolutionary.

So if you want to change your identity, pick something you've told yourself you "can't" do — and begin learning it. Not to prove yourself. Not to impress anyone. But to remind your nervous system that you are not finished. That you are a work in progress. That you have agency. That you are not frozen in time.

The moment you commit to learning, you signal to your brain: *We're becoming someone new.*

In the next section, we'll look at how this process builds real confidence — not the kind you perform for others, but the kind that lives in your bones. Because confidence, at its core, is not the absence of fear. It's the presence of competence — and the willingness to earn it.

The Confidence Loop

Most people misunderstand confidence. They think it's a personality trait — something you either have or don't. Or they see it as a performance: a loud voice, a firm handshake, a strong opinion. But real confidence has nothing to do with volume. It's not found in how you present yourself when the spotlight is on — it's built quietly, through a process that happens behind the scenes. Confidence is not the starting point. It's the outcome of a loop. And once you understand that loop, you can begin to generate confidence at will.

Here's how the confidence loop works:

You take action → You build capability → Capability builds confidence → Confidence makes future action easier.

It's a self-reinforcing cycle. But the loop doesn't start with belief — it starts with behavior. That's the part most people miss. They wait to *feel* confident before they act. But that's backward. Confidence is not a prerequisite for action. It's a *result* of action repeated enough times to create competence.

Think of anything you're good at now — something that feels natural or easy. At one point, it wasn't. You probably felt clumsy, uncertain, or nervous. But you kept showing up. You practiced. You learned. You improved. And slowly, what was once foreign became familiar. You began to trust yourself. That's confidence. Not because you decided to believe in yourself, but because you earned the right to. Through repetition. Through effort. Through engagement with reality.

But here's where the loop gets broken for many people: they try something once or twice, struggle, and conclude they're "just not good at it." That's not failure. That's *training*. Struggle is not the enemy of confidence — it's the soil it grows in. Every stumble, every awkward attempt, every imperfect start is part of the process. Confidence isn't about getting it right the first time. It's about proving to yourself that you can navigate the gap between not knowing and knowing — between fear and familiarity.

The loop also works in reverse. If you don't take action, you don't build capability. If you don't build capability, you won't feel competent. And without competence, confidence fades. The less confident you feel, the more likely you are to avoid taking action. And avoidance, over time, turns into a belief: *I'm just not that kind of person*. But it's not true. It's just a loop you never fully entered.

Once you see this, it becomes clear: you don't have to wait to be confident. You have to start the loop. Take the step. Send the message. Sign up for the thing. Go to the class. Ask for the feedback. Try, fail, try again. Every one of these acts builds capability. And with every small success, every moment of progress, your nervous system updates its assessment of who you are. *Maybe I can do this. Maybe I'm not bad at it. Maybe I'm getting better.*

And the best part? You don't need external validation to complete the loop. You don't need applause, followers, or approval. What you need is *evidence*. Evidence that you're growing. That you're learning. That you're taking steps in alignment with your future self. That's what confidence is built from — not perfection, but *proof*.

So if you want to feel more confident, stop focusing on how you feel and start focusing on what you do. Because the fastest way to build belief in yourself is to do the very thing you doubt — again and again — until it stops feeling like a risk and starts feeling like reality.

Let's make this practical. Next, you'll learn how to design a learning path — not just to acquire skills, but to reinforce the identity you're stepping into. Because when capability becomes intentional, identity becomes inevitable.

Designing a Capability Path

If you want to become someone new, you must learn to do things your current self doesn't yet know how to do. That's not a flaw — it's a requirement. Every version of you that lives closer to your goals, values, or vision will demand new capabilities. Not necessarily because the task is hard, but because it's *different*. And difference always feels difficult at first. This is why skill-building shouldn't be random or reactive. It should be *designed*. Because when you intentionally develop new capabilities in service of your identity, you create a path toward becoming someone you actually recognize and respect.

But most people approach growth passively. They wait to feel ready. They hope they'll be "called up" into the next version of their life. Or they stumble into competence by accident, through the friction of survival or circumstance. That kind of growth does happen—but it's chaotic. Disorganized. Painful. And often unsustainable. Intentional growth, on the other hand, is architectural. You choose the direction. You select the tools. You lay the foundation on purpose.

Start with a question: *Who am I becoming?* Be honest. Not who others expect you to be. Not who would impress the world. But the version of you who feels most aligned, most liberated, most fully alive. What does that version of you do that you don't yet know how to do? What do they say, practice, embody, or create? What skills come easily to them that currently feel out of reach for you?

Now flip those observations into a learning plan. Do you need to learn to speak with clarity and conviction? Study communication. Practice storytelling. Join a group that pushes you to use your voice. Do you want to lead a team, launch a business, or step into a more visible role? Learn decision-making, emotional regulation, time management, negotiation. Do you want deeper relationships? Study intimacy, vulnerability, empathy. Identify the capabilities that would unlock the identity you want to embody—and then build them, one layer at a time.

This doesn't mean you're becoming superhuman. You're simply removing the friction between your current skill set and your future self. You are collapsing the gap between *who you say you want to be* and *what you're actually prepared to handle*. And when you approach learning as identity reinforcement, every lesson becomes meaningful. Every practice session becomes proof. Every moment of progress becomes part of your story.

Structure matters. Your learning path should feel like a progression, not a guessing game. Break your capabilities into micro-skills. Identify resources: books, courses, mentors, communities. Set timelines. Schedule practice. Create feedback loops. Most of all, track your evolution—not just in terms of what you can do, but in how you now see yourself.

Because as your capability expands, so does your confidence. And as your confidence expands, so does your identity. Soon, you'll find yourself making decisions that your old self wouldn't have dared to consider. Not because you forced it—but because your skills caught up with your vision. You are no longer pretending. You are no longer rehearsing. You are becoming.

> "The outer conditions of a person's life will always be found to reflect their inner beliefs."
>
> -James Allen

CHAPTER 6

Beliefs – The Invisible Rules That Shape Who You're Allowed to Be

You don't see the word as it is. You see it as you believe it to be.

Your Brain is a Pattern-Making Machine

Every human being lives inside a world of meanings. We don't react to reality—we react to the *story* we believe about reality. That story is shaped by beliefs. Not just surface-level opinions, but deeply rooted internal rules that define what's possible, what's safe, what's right, and most of all—*who we're allowed to be.* These beliefs operate silently. They don't shout. They whisper. And yet, they shape everything: your confidence, your relationships, your decisions, your identity.

The brain is wired to find patterns. It does this for survival. If something happens once, it notices. If it happens again, it labels. If it keeps happening, it forms a belief. You touch a hot stove and burn your hand—you believe stoves are dangerous. That's useful. But the brain applies the same logic to emotional experience. You try to speak up in class and someone laughs. Your nervous system records: *Speaking up is unsafe.* You ask for help and get ignored. It tags that moment: *I can't depend on others.* You show emotion and get told to toughen up. It files it away: *Vulnerability equals weakness.*

These aren't conclusions. They're protective patterns. And once they're in place, your brain doesn't just remember them—it starts to *look for evidence* to confirm them. This is called confirmation bias, and it's one of the most powerful—and dangerous—features of the human mind. Once you believe something, you unconsciously filter the world to support that belief. You overlook data that contradicts it. You highlight anything that proves it right. And with every repetition, the belief grows stronger, more automatic, more unquestioned.

Eventually, you forget that it's a belief at all. It becomes your *reality*.

This is how people end up living inside invisible cages. Not because the world is hostile, but because the stories they inherited, absorbed, or constructed early in life are still running the show. You might believe you're not creative because a teacher once gave you a low grade on a drawing. You might believe you're not lovable because someone left. You might believe you're bad with money because your parents struggled. And you don't even realize that these aren't truths—they're *rules*. Internal laws that you didn't choose, but have obeyed for years.

The most insidious part? Beliefs like these don't just shape your behavior—they shape your identity. You start to say things like *I've never been good at that*, or *That's just not me*, or *I always mess things up*. These statements sound like facts, but they're really conclusions built from incomplete data. And the more you repeat them, the more your nervous system weaves them into your self-concept. You're not just someone who *experienced* rejection—you start believing you *are* someone who always will. You're not just someone who's made financial mistakes—you start believing you *are* financially incompetent.

This chapter is about breaking those rules.

Because beliefs, no matter how old or ingrained, are not facts. They are assumptions. And assumptions can be challenged, re-examined, and rewritten. But to do that, you have to be willing to question the very foundation you've been standing on. That takes courage. It takes honesty. And most of all, it takes the realization that if you want to live differently, you must believe differently.

Next, we'll demonstrate how limiting beliefs hide inside your language—particularly the phrase *"I can't because..."* You'll see how these invisible conclusions run your life, and you'll begin learning how to dismantle them, one assumption at a time.

I Can't Because...

There are few phrases more revealing than "I can't because..." On the surface, it sounds practical. Rational. Even responsible. But underneath it, there is often something far more powerful: a belief. A rule. A unconscious story that determines what is possible and what is off-limits—not because the world says so, but because *you* do. The real problem with the phrase "I can't" isn't that it limits your options. It's that it disguises itself as the *truth*.

When someone says, *"I can't leave this job because I have bills to pay,"* they might be speaking from circumstance—but often, there's something deeper. Something like *"I believe I won't succeed on my own,"* or *"I don't deserve more than this,"* or *"I need to stay small to stay safe."* When someone says, *"I can't open up in relationships because I've been hurt,"* that's not just emotional caution—it's a belief that pain equals danger, that vulnerability equals weakness, or that love will always lead to loss. These hidden narratives are rarely said out loud. But they direct the movie of your life just the same.

Limiting beliefs rarely start as conscious decisions. They often begin as protection. You failed once and felt shame, so your nervous system decided, *Never again.* You took a risk and got burned, so your unconscious concluded, *That's too dangerous.* And so, instead of trying again, you rewrote your life to avoid the risk altogether. You made your world smaller—but called it "realistic." You talked yourself out of trying—but called it "mature." You dismissed your desires—but called it "being practical."

We all do this. We all have areas in our lives where *"I can't because..."* has taken root, and we've stopped questioning it. It's easy to spot when someone else is doing it, but much harder to catch in yourself—because your version of "I can't" feels logical. Familiar. Unarguable. You've repeated it so many times, it no longer feels like a choice. It feels like a law of nature. But it's not. It's just a belief. One that can be challenged, revised, or completely discarded.

Here's the key: if the word "because" is followed by a circumstance, listen for the underlying assumption. Is it *really* about the external world? Or is it about an internal rule you've never questioned? Often, "I can't because I have kids" hides a belief like *I'm not allowed to prioritize myself.* "I can't because I'm too old" masks *It's too late for me to change.* "I can't because I don't know how" usually means *I don't trust myself to learn without failing.* When you surface the real belief beneath the surface excuse, you stop being a victim of your story—and start becoming the author of a new one.

Here's the practice: every time you hear yourself say or think, *"I can't because..."*, pause. Write it down. Then ask: *What do I actually believe this means about me? What am I afraid will happen if I do it anyway? Whose voice is this? And do I want to keep believing it?*

This process isn't about blindly ignoring reality. It's about reclaiming your authority over what's possible. Some things *are* hard. Some things *do* take time, energy, or sacrifice. But when you move from "I can't" to "I choose not to because..." you shift from powerlessness to authorship. You stop being controlled by unexamined beliefs—and start choosing your actions based on alignment, not fear.

And that, ultimately, is the difference between living a default life and an intentional one. The default life is governed by beliefs you didn't choose, based on experiences you didn't process, creating results you didn't want. An intentional life is different. It begins with radical self-honesty. It says, *If my actions are shaped by my beliefs, then my first job is to understand what I believe—and why.*

Next, we'll take a look at how your brain selectively gathers "evidence" to keep old beliefs alive, even when they no longer serve you. Because to build a new identity, you must not only question the rules—but stop feeding them the evidence they crave.

The Myth of Evidence

Beliefs don't sit idle. They hunt. They search for proof. They whisper, *"See? I told you so,"* every time something happens that fits the story they've been telling. This is why so many people feel stuck—not because they're lazy or unmotivated, but because their beliefs are actively reinforcing the limitations they're trying to escape. It's not just that you believe something. It's that you've spent years collecting "evidence" to confirm it, while ignoring anything that might contradict it.

This is the myth of evidence: the illusion that because something has happened before, it must continue to happen; that the past is a predictor of your identity, not just your history. You tried to launch a business and it didn't work—therefore, *"I'm not cut out to be an entrepreneur."* You got rejected after opening up—so you decided, *"People can't be trusted."* You've never been fit—so you believe, *"I'm just not an athletic person."* The mistake is not in noticing patterns. It's in treating them as permanent. But patterns are not prophecies. They are simply repetitions—often born from beliefs that caused the behavior in the first place.

Your mind is not neutral when it collects evidence. It's selective. And if a belief says *"You're not good enough,"* your brain will highlight every failure, every criticism, every sideways glance that might even remotely support that story. It will *ignore* the compliments, the wins, the progress. That's not you being negative—that's your brain doing its job. The problem is that your belief system is acting like a corrupt courtroom: the verdict was decided before the trial even began.

This is why so many people never break free. They don't realize they're living in a feedback loop. The belief causes the behavior. The behavior creates a result. The result reinforces the belief. And round and round it goes—until the belief feels like identity, and the story becomes indistinguishable from the self.

But there's a crack in this system—a way out. You can stop giving your beliefs the evidence they're demanding. You can start gathering *new* evidence. The kind that supports a different story. A better story. A *truer* story. You do this by acting *against* the belief, even when it feels unnatural. You reach out for connection, even if your belief says people will reject you. You try again, even when your belief says you'll fail. You speak up, even when your belief says no one's listening. And when the outcome doesn't match the old narrative, you pause—and you *notice*.

Most people miss this moment. They take a brave step, experience something new, but then dismiss it as a fluke. A lucky break. A one-off. Because if they accepted it as real, they'd have to confront the fact that their old belief might be wrong. And that's terrifying. Because if your old belief is wrong, what else might be possible?

The mind would rather be certain than free. It will cling to painful stories just to feel consistent. But your job, if you want to grow, is to choose freedom over certainty. You must be willing to say, *"Maybe what I've believed about myself isn't the full truth. Maybe I've been misinterpreting the data. Maybe it's time to collect better evidence."*

So here's your practice: start tracking small moments of contradiction. Times when someone appreciates you. Times when you try something and it goes well. Times when your default belief doesn't come true. Don't dismiss them. Don't explain them away. *Document* them. Use them as fuel to weaken the old story. Evidence is not static. It is renewable. You get to choose what you highlight. You get to decide which story gets reinforced.

Up next, we'll move from awareness to action. You'll learn how to *interrogate* a belief—how to take it off the pedestal and examine it with the honesty and precision of someone ready to change. Because beliefs can be stubborn, but they are not immune to questions.

How to Interrogate a Belief

Most people live with their beliefs the way someone might live with inherited furniture: it's been in the room so long, you forget you didn't choose it. You don't question whether it fits your life anymore—you just arrange everything around it. But beliefs are not heirlooms. They are tools. And tools must be examined, sharpened, sometimes discarded. If a belief is keeping you small, fearful, or stuck, it's time to interrogate it— not with shame, but with curiosity. Not to win an argument, but to reclaim your authority over what gets to live in your mind.

Interrogating a belief means pulling it out of the shadows and holding it up to the light. It means asking hard questions, the kind that make the belief squirm. Most beliefs, when finally confronted, turn out to be flimsy things—built on outdated data, vague fears, and conclusions drawn by a younger, more frightened version of you. The goal is not to attack yourself. The goal is to become someone who no longer mistakes an old wound for a permanent identity.

Start by identifying the belief clearly. Write it down. No editing. No justifying. No sugar-coating. Say what your nervous system actually believes. Not what you *want* to believe. Not what sounds good. But the quiet, painful statement that still lives in the background of your choices. *"I'm not lovable." "I'll never get ahead." "People always leave." "I'm not good enough."* It may sound dramatic. But you can't heal what you refuse to name.

Next, ask yourself: *Where did this belief come from?* Whose voice is this? Was it a parent, a teacher, a rejection, a trauma? Did you decide this after a single painful moment, or a series of disappointments? Did you absorb this from a culture that didn't see your value, or a system that rewarded you for playing small? Context matters. When you understand the emotional origin of a belief, you loosen its grip. You begin to see that it wasn't born from truth, but from adaptation.

Now, ask: *Is this belief universally true?* Could someone else, with the same background, believe something different? Have there been moments in my life that contradict this belief? What am I ignoring to keep it alive? This is where the cracks begin to form. Because very few beliefs—especially the self-limiting kind—can withstand sustained questioning. They were built for speed, not scrutiny. They exist to keep you safe, not fulfilled.

Then ask: *What is this belief costing me?* How has it shaped my decisions? What opportunities has it talked me out of? What relationships has it weakened? What dreams has it delayed or destroyed? This is where the pain becomes clarity. You realize that carrying the belief isn't just uncomfortable—it's expensive. It's stealing your time, your peace, your potential.

Finally, ask: *What might be a more empowering belief?* Not a fantasy. Not blind optimism. But a new assumption that honors your experience while opening up possibility. *"I'm not broken—I'm in progress." "I've failed before, and I've also grown." "I'm allowed to change."* A belief doesn't need to be perfect to be powerful. It just needs to move you in the direction of who you want to become.

Interrogating a belief is not a one-time event. It's a habit. A discipline. A way of relating to your own mind with maturity and respect. Because you are not your thoughts. You are the thinker. And the thinker has the power to rewrite the script.

In the next section, we'll complete this chapter by exploring how to *install* upgraded beliefs—deliberately and strategically—so they become more than words. They become architecture for your identity. Because when your beliefs change, your behavior follows. And when your behavior changes, your life does too.

Installing Upgraded Beliefs

Once you've dismantled a limiting belief, you stand in unfamiliar territory. There's space now—raw, open space where an old story used to live. For many people, this is where they stop. They feel relief from the weight of their former belief but don't yet know what to build in its place. And like a house without a frame, an unstructured mind will default to old construction. If you want lasting transformation, the work doesn't end with breaking beliefs. You must replace them with something stronger. Something that can hold the weight of your next identity. You must *install* new beliefs—on purpose.

But new beliefs aren't adopted by declaration. You don't just say, "I believe in myself now," and expect your unconscious to fall in line. The mind doesn't respond to slogans. It responds to *evidence, repetition, and emotional intensity*. So if you want a new belief to take root, you must treat it like a seed. You plant it. You water it. You reinforce it through daily behavior. And you protect it—especially in the beginning—because nothing is more fragile than a belief you've never lived before.

Start by crafting the upgraded belief in a way that feels empowering but believable. It should stretch you—not snap you. If your old belief was *"I always mess things up,"* don't jump straight to *"I'm flawless and unstoppable."* Your nervous system will reject it as false. Instead, try *"I'm learning to handle things with more clarity and care,"* or *"Even when I stumble, I move forward."* The key is *emotional credibility*. The belief must feel like something you can *try on*, even if it's not yet fully yours.

Then, tie this belief to behavior. Don't wait to feel it— *live* it. If your new belief is *"My voice matters,"* speak up. Share your perspective. Start a conversation you'd usually avoid. If your new belief is *"I'm capable of growth,"* engage in learning. Take the class. Try the thing. Every time you act in alignment with your upgraded belief, you send a message to your nervous system: *This is who we are now*. That's how identity begins to shift—not through thought alone, but through congruent action repeated over time.

Use repetition. Create rituals. Write your new belief daily. Speak it out loud in the mirror. Journal about how you lived it each day. Anchor it in your environment—post it on your wall, your phone, your workspace. When you forget it (and you will), gently return to it. Don't punish yourself for slipping. That's part of rewiring. You're not just memorizing a sentence—you're rewiring your sense of self. That takes time. And it's worth it.

Use emotional intensity. Connect the new belief to a vision, a value, a memory that matters. Think of someone you love. Think of the life you want to live. Think of the moment you said, *"Enough."* Emotion helps the mind encode new patterns more deeply. It makes the belief feel urgent, not optional.

Finally, surround yourself with people who reflect the belief back to you. Identity is social. If you're trying to believe you're creative, hang around people who value and support creativity. If you're trying to believe you're capable of leadership, find spaces where you're treated as someone with influence. The right community doesn't just support your new belief—they *accelerate* it.

And if you don't have that community yet, be that mirror for yourself. Review your wins. Track your progress.

Remind yourself daily: *I am not who I was. I am who I'm becoming.*

Because belief is not just about accuracy—it's about alignment. You don't need beliefs that are objectively provable. You need beliefs that *serve* you. That move you. That make your future self possible. And when you choose them wisely—and reinforce them relentlessly—you don't just change how you think. You change who you are.

"Beliefs are not truths – they are agreements you made with yourself when you were too young to question them. Now you know better. Now you choose."

-Keith Leonard

"The strongest force in the human personality is the need to stay consistent with how we define ourselves."

-Tony Robbins

CHAPTER 7

The Identity Operating System

Who you are is not something you find. It's something you build.

Identity is a Decision, Not a Discovery

For most of your life, you've been told to "find yourself." As if the real you is hidden somewhere—beneath a pile of mistakes, or inside a job title, or buried in a childhood memory. And so you search. You journal, reflect, talk to friends, meditate, even travel across the world, hoping that some experience or moment will finally reveal who you *really* are. But the reality is: **identity is not found. It is forged.** The self isn't something waiting to be uncovered. It's something you actively create.

This idea may feel strange at first. Especially if you've spent years treating identity like a fixed essence—something shaped by your past, inherited from your family, or discovered through introspection. But identity isn't a set of personality traits, or a birthright, or a psychological label. Identity is a choice. A design. An operating system you decide to run your life on—consciously or unconsciously. And just like any system, it can be reprogrammed.

Think of your current identity as a default setting. It wasn't maliciously installed, but it wasn't intentionally chosen either. You picked up pieces from the people around you: the child who learned not to take up space, the teenager who became "the funny one" to stay safe, the adult who overdelivers because somewhere deep down they don't feel like enough. These roles worked at some point. They kept you included. Protected. Praised. But now? They may be outdated. Misaligned. Or flat-out false.

And yet, most people continue to live inside these versions of themselves because it feels *true*. But here's the catch: just because something feels true doesn't mean it *is*. It just means it's familiar. And familiarity is not a good enough reason to keep living a story that no longer reflects who you're becoming.

The breakthrough begins when you realize that identity isn't something you wait to discover—**it's something you declare.** You say, *This is who I am now*. Not as a performance. Not as a fantasy. But as an act of creative responsibility. You choose who you want to be, and then you begin to align your life with that decision—not instantly, but consistently.

Of course, it won't feel real right away. That's okay. Identity doesn't need immediate proof to begin shaping you. It needs commitment. Repetition. And time. Just like any decision worth making. When you adopt a new identity, you are rewriting your internal source code. You are choosing new rules for what you believe, how you act, and what you allow yourself to experience. You are upgrading your self-concept to match the future you're creating—not the past you survived.

This doesn't mean you abandon your history. It means you no longer let your history dictate your possibilities. You honor the past. You learn from it. And then, you evolve beyond it. Because the moment you decide who you are now—*really decide*—you stop needing to be validated by what came before. You become someone new. Not in theory. In behavior. In voice. In presence. In outcome.

What we'll do next is look at how your self-labels become self-fulfilling prophecies. Because once you declare an identity, your brain begins to build a world around it. The question is: are you building that world on purpose—or by default?

The "I Am" Loop

The most powerful words in the human language are "I am." Not because of what follows them, but because of what they *create*. Every time you say, *"I am this,"* or *"I am not that,"* you are building a blueprint for how you're allowed to think, act, feel, relate, and respond. You're programming your internal operating system. And once that code is written, everything you do will loop back to reinforce it—*especially if you're not paying attention.*

This is the "I Am" loop: a self-fulfilling cycle where your identity drives your actions, and your actions reinforce your identity. It's subtle, but powerful. If you say, *"I'm not good with people,"* you'll avoid social situations. If you say, *"I'm just not a leader,"* you'll stay quiet when your voice is needed. If you say, *"I've always been anxious,"* you'll interpret every flutter of uncertainty as confirmation. These "I am" statements aren't just observations. They are instructions. And your brain follows them with precision.

What makes the loop so potent is that once you've said it enough times, your nervous system stops questioning it. It simply *obeys*. It pulls your attention toward things that validate the label and filters out anything that contradicts it. This is why change is so hard—not because people lack the ability to act differently, but because their "I am" statements won't *let* them. They try to build a new life while silently repeating an old identity. And that identity—quietly, consistently—undoes every step forward.

But here's the truth most people don't realize: your "I am" statements were never facts. They were decisions. Some were made intentionally. Most were made in moments of pain, fear, or confusion. You said, *"I guess I'm just not that kind of person,"* after failing once. You said, *"I'm not meant for more,"* when someone rejected you. You said, *"I'm not the type who speaks up,"* because doing so once got you hurt. But those weren't conclusions. They were *coping mechanisms*. Temporary shields that hardened into permanent beliefs.

The good news? Anything installed can be uninstalled. The loop can be broken—but only when you become conscious of it. That's your first step. Begin noticing every time you say or think "I am." Say it out loud. Listen to it in your self-talk. Catch it in your writing, your excuses, your stories. Don't judge it. Just observe. What patterns do you find? Which "I am"s are keeping you anchored in a smaller version of your life?

Then, ask yourself: *Who gave me this identity? Did I choose this—or did I inherit it?* Trace the origin. Did someone else call you lazy, quiet, intense, dramatic, forgetful, too much, too little? Did you accept that label because it helped you fit in—or stay out of trouble? What has that identity cost you? And what might become possible if you decided to write something new?

Here's what's revolutionary: you don't need permission to change your "I am." You don't need evidence in advance. You don't even need to feel ready. You just need to choose a better loop. One that supports your vision. One that aligns with the kind of person you're becoming, not the kind of person you used to be.

Start with a single line. Not a performance. Not a wish. But a declaration. *"I am learning to lead." "I am the kind of person who shows up." "I am someone who honors their word." "I am becoming someone who trusts themselves."* And then act accordingly. Even when it feels awkward. Especially when it feels awkward. Because the loop gets stronger with use. And each time you act in alignment with a new "I am," you reinforce a new self.

You don't have to wait for proof to start believing. You create proof by choosing who you are—and then living like it's already true.

Now, let us examine how these identity declarations don't just change your behavior—they change the *way you see reality*. Because once you change your "I am," the world around you begins to shift in kind.

How Identity Reinvents Reality

We like to think we see the world as it is. Rationally. Clearly. Objectively. But we don't. We see the world through a filter—a lens colored by who we believe ourselves to be. And that filter changes everything. Two people can walk into the same room, hear the same comment, face the same challenge, and have radically different reactions—not because reality is different, but because their *identities* are. One feels insulted, the other motivated. One sees an opportunity, the other a threat. Identity is not just personal—it's perceptual. It shapes the meaning you assign to everything.

If you believe you're a survivor, you'll see hard times as confirmation of your strength. If you believe you're a victim, you'll see the same events as proof that life is against you. If you believe you're a leader, you'll interpret problems as your responsibility to solve. If you believe you're invisible, you'll assume no one's listening. It's not the event that determines your experience—it's the *identity* running your interpretation of it. And that interpretation becomes your reality.

This is why identity work isn't just internal—it's transformational. When you upgrade your identity, you don't just act differently. You *see* differently. The room changes. The options change. The people you notice change. The way you respond to failure, feedback, even your own thoughts—it all shifts. Because you're not looking through the same lens anymore. You're not living in the same internal world.

Let's say you once saw yourself as "the quiet one." That identity became a filter. In conversations, you'd scan for moments to retreat. You'd assume people weren't interested in your input. You'd ignore invitations to speak, waiting for permission that never came. And so, you'd stay quiet—not because you lacked something to say, but because your *identity* told you silence was safer. Now, let's say you begin to shift. You start seeing yourself as "someone who adds value in conversations." Suddenly, the same environment feels different. You're more alert to when your voice is needed. You frame your ideas as contributions, not disruptions. And when someone nods in agreement, you *notice*. The world didn't change. *You* did. And that changed *everything*.

We don't act to confirm what's true. We act to confirm who we are. Your identity seeks alignment, and it will shape your reality to get it. If your identity says you're not worthy of success, you'll unconsciously sabotage opportunities—then point to the outcome as "proof." If your identity says you're resilient, you'll bounce back from setbacks faster—then use that as evidence of your strength. The loop is always active. The question is: *Are you using it consciously, or letting it use you?*

To change your reality, you don't need to manipulate the outside world. You need to change the identity through which you *perceive* it. You need to stop asking, "What do I do?" and start asking, "Who am I being when I do it?" That shift—from behavior to being—alters the lens. And once the lens shifts, so do the possibilities.

This is why some people seem to grow exponentially. It's not just that they work harder. It's that they *live* from a different identity—one that allows them to interpret, act, and recover at a higher level. They don't see failure as a signal to stop. They see it as a normal part of becoming who they've already decided to be. Their self-concept is so aligned with their vision that setbacks don't unravel them—they reinforce them.

Identity is not just who you are. It's the *way* you interpret life. And when you shift the interpreter, everything you experience begins to transform. What once felt threatening now feels like a test. What once felt impossible becomes your next stretch. What once felt like "just the way things are" becomes *negotiable*.

Next, we'll discuss why changing your identity doesn't just feel like growth—it can also feel like grief. Because becoming someone new requires letting go of who you've been. And that goodbye, if left unspoken, can quietly sabotage your progress.

The Death of the Old Self

There's a hidden cost to transformation that nobody talks about—one that can sneak up on even the most committed person doing deep inner work. It's not exhaustion, or discipline, or even fear. It's *grief*. Because when you change who you are, you inevitably have to let go of who you've been. And even if that old identity kept you small, scared, or misaligned, it also kept you *safe*. It helped you survive. It gave you rules to follow. It was familiar. And letting it go can feel like a kind of death.

Most people don't realize how attached they are to the self they're trying to outgrow. They focus on their goals—what they want to do, what they want to achieve—but they forget that real change requires releasing the patterns, protections, and roles that once defined them. You can't carry an outdated self into an upgraded life. That's not evolution—it's emotional hoarding. And at some point, that weight will break you or block you.

You might not even notice the grief at first. It can show up as hesitation, procrastination, or self-sabotage. You'll inch toward the edge of transformation, then pull back—not because the new identity isn't exciting, but because the old one is *unfinished*. Unprocessed. Unmourned. And a part of you still wants to keep it alive. After all, the self you're letting go of got you here. Maybe it was the overachiever who earned the praise. The caretaker who made sure everyone else was okay. The rebel who refused to be controlled. The perfectionist who thought being flawless would make them lovable. That version of you had a purpose. And burying it without acknowledgment can feel like betrayal.

So don't skip the funeral. If you want to move forward fully, you need to honor the identity you're leaving behind. Thank it. Bless it. Write it a letter if you have to. Not because it was your truth—but because it was your *strategy*. It helped you navigate a world that didn't always see you clearly. It taught you lessons, revealed your strengths, and protected your most tender parts. You don't have to carry it with you to be grateful for what it gave you.

Grief is not a sign you're doing it wrong. It's a signal that something real is happening. You're shedding old skin. Closing a chapter. Ending a performance. And there's sadness in that—even when it's healthy. But there's also *power*. Because once you've made peace with who you were, you're free to become someone new without guilt. Without second-guessing. Without negotiating your next level with a past that no longer defines you.

This is why transformation often feels like a paradox. You're becoming more *you* than ever before—yet losing parts of yourself in the process. That's not failure.

That's *metamorphosis*. The caterpillar isn't wrong for dissolving. It's the only way it can fly.

Give yourself permission to feel the full spectrum of change—not just the clarity and confidence, but the confusion, the nostalgia, the release. And when the old self comes knocking, as it inevitably will, whisper gently: *Thank you. I don't need you anymore.* Then turn your attention to the identity you're constructing, because your future deserves your full presence.

Now, let's take that presence and put it to work. Up next, you'll learn how to *intentionally construct* your Identity 2.0—rooted not in fear or familiarity, but in chosen values and vision. Because once you've made room by letting go, you get to rebuild with intention.

Constructing Identity 2.0

Now that the old self has been honored and released, the real work begins. Because transformation isn't just subtraction—it's construction. You're not just removing what no longer fits; you're *building* who you choose to become. And this is the most sacred act of identity work: to deliberately, courageously, and creatively craft a self that aligns with your deepest values, not your oldest fears.

Constructing Identity 2.0 starts with a question that sounds simple but is anything but: *Who am I when I'm no longer performing for approval, reacting to pain, or protecting old wounds?* Most people don't have a ready answer. That's okay. You're not expected to have a fully formed vision. But what you *must* have is a willingness to imagine. A willingness to name the qualities, traits, and values of the person you'd be if you weren't bound by history or habit. Not a fantasy self. Not a perfect self. A *purposeful* one.

Begin with values, not outcomes. Most people try to build their identity around what they want to achieve—money, fitness, status, relationships. But outcomes are fragile. They can be lost, delayed, or disrupted. A true identity is built on principles you can live every day, regardless of what happens. Ask yourself: *What matters to me more than comfort? What qualities do I want to embody in every interaction? What traits feel like home—not because they're easy, but because they're true?* Maybe it's integrity. Maybe it's courage. Maybe it's presence, creativity, resilience, devotion. These become the cornerstones of your construction.

From there, translate values into *traits*. If you value courage, what does that look like in action? How does a courageous version of you speak, walk, make decisions, set boundaries? If you value compassion, how does that show up in your relationships, your self-talk, your leadership? Every trait you choose becomes a building block. Together, they form a coherent, lived identity—not a costume, but a foundation.

Now give that identity a name. Not a title or a job description—but a phrase that anchors your new way of being. It might be simple: *The Grounded Leader. The Bold Creator. The Calm Presence.* Or more vivid: *The One Who Speaks with Fire and Listens with Grace.* This is your internal North Star—not for others to see, but for you to return to when life gets loud. It's your declaration. Your compass. Your architecture.

Then you test it. You live it. Not perfectly—but consistently. You ask, *What does this version of me do next?* You build micro-evidence. You use behavior to reinforce belief. You stretch when it's easier to shrink. You respond from identity, not emotion. And when you forget—when the old self creeps back in—you don't collapse. You remember that this new identity isn't a mask. It's a choice. And you can choose it again, and again, and again, until it feels like home.

One of the greatest lies of personal growth is that change is a straight line. It's not. It's a spiral. You'll revisit the same patterns, but from new heights. You'll be tested, not to punish you, but to strengthen your foundation. And every time you return to your chosen self—even after slipping—you reinforce that this is who you are *now*. Not because of your past. But because of your *decision*.

Constructing Identity 2.0 isn't a one-time event. It's a relationship—a commitment to become the person you're proud to live as. And as that identity takes root, the world begins to reorganize around you. New opportunities, deeper relationships, more honest conversations, more aligned decisions. Not because you forced them. But because you finally *matched* your outer world to your inner truth.

This is your power. You are the builder, the architect, and the inhabitant of your identity. And from here forward, every moment becomes a construction site for your future self.

> "When you live with purpose, you don't have to chase happiness or significance – it finds you."
>
> -Dr. Cloé Madanes

CHAPTER 8

Purpose and Spiritual Congruence

Your identity becomes magnetic when it serves something greater than self.

You Are More Than Productivity

Somewhere along the way, your worth got tangled up with your usefulness. You began to believe that what made you valuable was your output—your ability to produce, to deliver, to achieve. Maybe it started in school, where performance was measured in grades and gold stars. Or in your family, where you felt noticed only when you were excelling or behaving. Or in the workplace, where your presence seemed to matter most when it was tied to results. Wherever it began, it taught you this: you are what you *do*. And the more you do, the more you matter.

This belief is so common, so deeply woven into our culture, that it often goes unquestioned. We wear our busyness like a badge. We brag about early mornings and late nights. We chase success not just for what it can give us, but for what it can *say* about us. In a world addicted to measurement, we confuse *productivity* with *purpose*. But they're not the same. Productivity is about output. Purpose is about *alignment*. And until you learn to separate the two, your identity will be tethered to performance in a way that leaves you anxious, empty, or both.

Here's the truth: you are not here to simply perform. You are here to *become*. And becoming cannot be measured by how many emails you answer, how many goals you hit, or how many plates you keep spinning. Becoming is measured in alignment—how closely your daily actions, your internal compass, and your deeper sense of meaning reflect one another. When these align, you feel alive. When they don't, even your biggest accomplishments feel strangely hollow.

Many high performers hit this wall. They wake up one day with all the trappings of success—the job, the income, the admiration—and feel like they're living someone else's life. That's not because they didn't work hard. It's because their work was built on identity 1.0—an outdated self, chasing validation through effort. They were climbing fast, but the ladder was leaning on the wrong wall. And no amount of success can fill the space where *meaning* is supposed to live.

That's where purpose comes in. Not as a dramatic life mission or Instagram-worthy passion, but as a quiet, steady alignment between *who you are* and *why it matters*. Purpose is what gives weight to your identity. It's what keeps your new self from feeling like a costume. It transforms your daily efforts from a grind into a contribution. Without it, transformation stays self-centered—focused only on becoming more confident, more capable, more successful. But with it? It becomes service-centered. And that's where identity becomes transcendent.

To step into Identity 2.0, you must ask a deeper question: *What is all of this for?* Not in a guilt-driven, moralistic way—but in an expansive, soulful way. Who benefits from you becoming this version of yourself? Whose life is elevated by your evolution? What would the world lose if you played small? These are not abstract spiritual inquiries. They are the heart of a sustainable identity. Because when your growth feeds more than just your ego, you *keep going*—even when it's hard. Even when no one's watching. Even when the old patterns whisper you back into comfort.

You were not meant to live your life in service of a spreadsheet. You were meant to create, to love, to connect, to lead, to build something that matters. You were meant to live as someone whose existence *ripples*. And when you construct your identity around that ripple—when you wake up each day asking not just *what can I do,* but *who can I impact*—you start to feel the difference between a life that's productive and a life that's *on purpose.*

Up next, you'll learn how to anchor that purpose in meaning, not metrics—so your identity can stand strong even when the outcomes fluctuate, and your progress becomes harder to measure.

Meaning Before Metrics

In a world obsessed with measurement, it's easy to confuse *progress* with *purpose*. We track our steps, our sales, our followers, our calories, our inboxes. We tally our wins and flag our failures, often before the dust has even settled. We've been trained to believe that if something can't be measured, it doesn't count. But here's the quiet truth that most high achievers eventually discover: *the most important parts of your life will never fit in a spreadsheet.*

You can't measure the moment you truly forgave someone. You can't quantify the peace of knowing you finally spoke your truth. There is no dashboard for how deeply you listened to your child, or how much courage it took to show up to that difficult conversation, or how much grace you extended to yourself when you didn't have it all together. Yet these are the very moments that shape your identity. These are the shifts that define who you're becoming. And if you only chase what can be tracked, you'll miss the deeper transformation.

This is the trap of metrics-driven living: it trains you to prioritize what is *visible* over what is *valuable*. It tempts you to build a life that looks good in pictures but feels hollow on the inside. It rewards urgency over depth, hustle over harmony. But identity doesn't grow in the glare of metrics. It grows in the unseen places—when you say yes to your values even when no one is watching, when you turn inward for guidance instead of outward for applause.

This doesn't mean metrics are bad. Feedback is useful. Goals are motivating. Milestones are real. But they are not the *meaning*. They are not the identity. They are simply indicators. The danger comes when we build our self-concept on numbers instead of *noticing*—noticing how aligned we feel, how much integrity we're living with, how authentically we're showing up in the world. Metrics can tell you what you're doing. Only *meaning* can tell you who you're becoming.

Here's a simple but radical shift: what if you tracked alignment as carefully as you tracked outcomes? What if you checked in daily, not just on your progress, but on your *presence*? Did I act like the person I say I'm becoming today? Did I bring my values into the room? Did I honor the deeper why behind my actions—or just chase another gold star?

Meaning makes your identity resilient. Without it, the moment you fall behind, miss a goal, or get overlooked, your entire sense of self starts to shake. But when your identity is built on a purpose bigger than performance, you stay grounded. You know who you are, even when the numbers fluctuate. You measure your days not just in wins, but in alignment. And that creates a different kind of success—one that feels like integrity instead of pressure.

In a culture that wants you to prove your worth, choosing meaning is an act of rebellion. It's how you take back your inner compass. It's how you keep your identity sacred in a world that keeps trying to sell you someone else's version of success.

Coming up, we'll explore what it looks like to live with that inner compass fully turned on—to develop a sense of direction that comes not from ego, but from something deeper, more enduring, and soul-rooted.

The Soul-Level Compass

There is a kind of knowing that doesn't come from logic, data, or approval. It lives deeper than thought—beneath the strategies, beneath the productivity, beneath even your best intentions. It's not loud or urgent. In fact, it often whispers. But when you learn to listen to it, your entire life begins to move in alignment. This is your soul-level compass—the quiet, unwavering inner signal that points you toward who you truly are, and who you are here to become.

Most people override this compass without even realizing it. They've been trained to trust outer signals more than inner ones. The expectations of others. The rules of their industry. The speed of their peers. They move toward what looks successful, what seems impressive, or what feels safest. And in doing so, they slowly drift away from what feels *right*. That's the dissonance so many high-functioning people feel—the invisible gap between achievement and aliveness.

Your soul doesn't care about your résumé. It cares about your *resonance*. About how it feels to be you at the end of the day, when the noise dies down and there's no one left to impress. When you are deeply aligned, there's a kind of internal click. You feel it not just in your head, but in your body. You speak and your voice doesn't shake. You move and your actions feel clean. You say yes, and it's a full-bodied yes. You say no, and it's a grounded, unapologetic no. This is not arrogance. This is congruence. The rare and powerful state where your thoughts, feelings, values, and actions are all on the same page.

This kind of congruence can't be faked. And it can't be downloaded from someone else's path. It must be cultivated—through deep listening, radical honesty, and a willingness to disappoint the world if it means staying true to your inner direction. That's not easy. Because there will always be voices—internal and external—urging you to play it safer, smaller, louder, faster. But your soul doesn't speak in volume. It speaks in *clarity*. And once you start building your identity around that clarity, life begins to simplify. Not because it gets easier, but because you stop arguing with yourself.

When your identity is rooted in this soul-level compass, everything shifts. You stop asking, "What should I do?" and start asking, "What aligns with who I'm here to become?" You stop chasing strategies and start following *integrity*. And even when you're scared, even when you don't know how it's going to turn out, you trust your feet. Because they're pointed in a direction that *feels* like home—even if the path ahead is unfamiliar.

This is not about being perfect. It's about being *whole*. When you live from the inside out, your identity becomes less about image and more about essence. You're no longer building a brand. You're becoming a presence. You stop being defined by your titles, your roles, your outcomes—and start being defined by the *energy* you bring into every room. The way people feel in your presence. The way you treat others when no one's watching. The way you treat yourself in the quiet moments. These are the markers of a spiritually congruent identity.

And this is the gift: the more aligned you are internally, the less you need external control. You stop forcing things. You stop gripping outcomes. You move with a kind of grounded confidence that can't be faked or taken away. Because it's not based on what you *do*. It's based on who you've *become*.

Now, let's take a look at how this shift leads to a profound reorientation—from trying to control your world, to contributing to it. Because once you're anchored in who you are, your attention expands from personal transformation to meaningful service.

Contribution, Not Control

There comes a point in personal growth when the work stops being about *you*. Not because you're finished evolving, but because something in you opens—and you realize that the most powerful identity isn't the one trying to *control* the world. It's the one that wants to *contribute* to it. Up until now, much of your transformation may have been understandably self-focused. Healing wounds. Building confidence. Letting go of patterns. Redesigning your life. That work matters. But identity reaches a new level of depth and durability when it becomes a vehicle for *service*.

This doesn't mean abandoning your dreams or becoming a martyr. It means understanding that your growth isn't just for your benefit. It's for the benefit of everyone your life touches. The courage you build inspires others to take their own leaps. The presence you embody helps others feel seen. The healing you've done allows you to break cycles instead of repeating them. When you begin to see your identity as a tool for contribution—not just a project for self-improvement—you unlock a different kind of power. Quiet. Steady. Enduring.

Most people, without realizing it, try to control their lives into significance. They chase titles, manipulate outcomes, obsess over image. They want their transformation to *guarantee* a result. But that's not transformation. That's bargaining. Real identity work is not a contract with the universe that says, "If I grow, I deserve comfort." It's a commitment that says, "Even if no one notices, even if nothing changes overnight, I will keep showing up as who I've decided to be." Why? Because that decision isn't based on fear anymore. It's based on *love*. For your own becoming. And for what your becoming makes possible for others.

When you stop trying to control and start choosing to contribute, something radical happens: you become *lighter*. More free. Your sense of worth no longer rises and falls with outcomes. You don't need to force every conversation, orchestrate every win, or cling to every plan. You live in alignment, and that alignment becomes your offering. Your energy, your choices, your attention—they become part of something bigger than your personal success. They become part of your *legacy*.

This is how Identity 2.0 becomes sustainable. Not through hustle. Through *meaningful generosity*. You shift your question from "How do I get what I want?" to "How do I serve what I'm here for?" And that shift changes everything. It makes you more magnetic. More trusted. More authentic. People can feel when your identity is no longer a performance. They respond not just to your words, but to the clarity of your presence. They're drawn to you—not because you're perfect, but because you're *true*.

And when setbacks come, when life gets messy or uncertain, you won't collapse. You'll remember that you weren't building this identity to control outcomes—you were building it to make a contribution. And that contribution continues, even when results are delayed. Even when others don't understand. Even when it's inconvenient.

Contribution doesn't always mean grand gestures. Sometimes it's your calm in the middle of someone else's storm. Sometimes it's your boundaries that model self-respect. Sometimes it's the way you show up on the hard days—honest, imperfect, human. All of it counts. All of it matters. Because when your identity is grounded in giving instead of gripping, your life becomes a source of strength—not just for you, but for the world around you.

As we wrap up this chapter, we'll experience what happens when all of this comes together—when your identity, your actions, your values, and your purpose align so fully that your life becomes magnetic. Not in the attention-seeking sense, but in the quietly powerful sense of a life that *pulls people forward* by its very presence.

A Life Worth Believing In

When all the layers come together—when your actions reflect your values, when your beliefs support your growth, when your identity aligns with your integrity, and your purpose extends beyond yourself—you begin to experience something rare and beautiful: a life that feels *whole*. Not perfect. Not always easy. But real. Integrated. Alive. This is what it means to live a life worth believing in. One where you no longer have to convince yourself you're on the right path because *everything in you* knows you are.

You don't need to have all the answers. You begin by creating a daily rhythm that makes you feel proud to be who you are. A way of living that doesn't require an audience to feel meaningful. A sense of self that no longer relies on outcomes to feel valid. You wake up in the morning with a quiet kind of conviction—not because you've mastered life, but because you're no longer at war with yourself. You've stopped pretending.

You've stopped performing. You've started *living as someone you trust.*

And that trust changes the way you move through the world. It gives you a voice that doesn't shake when you speak what matters. It gives you clarity that doesn't waver when others question your path. It gives you strength that isn't brittle, because it's not based on dominance—it's based on *alignment.* You no longer need to win every battle, because you're no longer trying to prove your identity. You're simply expressing it.

A life worth believing in is not built overnight. It's built in the moment-to-moment choices: the decision to act from purpose rather than pattern. The courage to say no to what's convenient in order to say yes to what's true. The discipline to hold your identity steady when old versions of you come knocking. And above all, the willingness to keep refining—not because you're broken, but because your identity is a living system. A sacred evolution. A relationship with yourself that grows deeper as you grow wiser.

When your identity is in alignment with your purpose, your presence becomes a form of leadership. You start to model what's possible—not by pushing, but by *being.* You become the kind of person who doesn't just talk about transformation, but lives it—subtly, consistently, powerfully. People feel it. And often, they rise just by being near you. That's not magic. That's integrity made visible.

This is the invitation of Identity 2.0—not to reinvent yourself once, but to live in a way that allows for constant recalibration. A way of being that honors where you've come from, celebrates where you're headed, and serves something bigger than your own comfort. It's a way of life that doesn't need to be validated—because it's already felt. By you. By the people around you. And by the world you're quietly impacting every day.

In the next chapter, we'll explore how to *live* this new identity—day in and day out—through integration, resilience, and the sacred rituals that turn alignment into embodiment. Because becoming Identity 2.0 is only the beginning. Now it's time to *live it*.

> "We don't rise to the levels of our goals, we fall to the level of our systems."
>
> —James Clear

CHAPTER 9

Living as Identity 2.0

Identity alignment is not a one-time breakthrough – it's a lifelong embodiment.

Integration Over Inspiration

The moment you begin to embody a new identity, something subtle but profound happens: the gap between who you've been and who you're becoming begins to close. It's no longer just about insight, or clarity, or those breathtaking moments of breakthrough where everything clicks. It's about *living it*—daily, deliberately, and in alignment with the version of yourself you've chosen. Because inspiration may spark transformation, but it's *integration* that sustains it.

Most people chase transformation like a peak experience. They want the high of the realization, the adrenaline of the insight. They want to feel changed. But what they often overlook is that the real shift happens *after* the breakthrough. In the quiet moments. In the way you structure your day. In how you speak when you're tired. In how you respond when you're challenged, when you're alone, when no one's watching. That's where identity gets solidified—not in the vision, but in the *repetition*.

This is where the work matures. You've done the excavation. You've reimagined who you are and why you're here. But to truly live as Identity 2.0, you must let that identity shape the structure of your life. Not as a temporary commitment, but as a daily practice. This means designing your environment to support the new self. It means tracking not just tasks, but alignment. It means staying conscious—especially in the mundane, repetitive spaces where the old identity used to take over without your permission.

Integration is the art of choosing your identity again and again until it becomes automatic—not because you're forcing it, but because it now *fits*. It's the difference between wearing a costume and wearing your own skin. It requires presence. It requires patience. And it requires compassion for yourself on the days when you slip, because those days are part of the process. Integration doesn't demand perfection. It demands *returning*.

This is where most people fall off—not because they don't want to change, but because they don't realize that transformation isn't a one-time decision. It's a way of life. It's saying, "This is who I am now," and letting that statement guide how you think, speak, plan, relate, rest, work, and lead. It's learning to love the rhythm of consistency more than the rush of reinvention. And it's understanding that your identity isn't a brand to manage—it's a foundation to *live from*.

When you integrate your identity fully, you start to feel a shift in your baseline. You wake up differently. You move through challenges differently. You recover faster. You relate more honestly. You find yourself thinking thoughts and making choices that match the person you set out to become—and not because you're trying. Because it's *who you are now*.

But make no mistake: living in this alignment doesn't eliminate difficulty. If anything, it asks more of you. It asks you to stay awake in your own life. To hold your new standard, not out of pressure, but out of self-respect. It asks you to become a guardian of your own congruence—not rigidly, but consciously. It's not always comfortable, but it is *clarifying*. You begin to recognize the difference between an old pattern and a new path. You become quicker to realign when you've drifted. And you feel the cost of misalignment not as guilt, but as a gentle nudge from your wiser self saying, "You know better now. Come back."

That return is the heart of integration. Not dramatic. Not public. Often not even seen. But deeply powerful. Because it's in that return—day after day, decision after decision—that Identity 2.0 is no longer something you're chasing. It's something you *embody*.

The Danger of Regression

No matter how strong your commitment, how vivid your vision, or how powerfully your Identity 2.0 has taken root, there will come a moment—perhaps many—when the old version of you resurfaces. Not because you've failed. Not because you weren't ready. But because transformation is not linear. Growth will always awaken resistance. And under pressure, the most familiar self is often the first one to answer the call.

Regression isn't always dramatic. Sometimes it's subtle—an old tone of voice, a default habit, a shrinking of your shoulders in a room where you promised yourself you'd stand tall. Other times, it's more blatant—a full reversion to behavior you thought you'd outgrown, triggered by stress, exhaustion, or unexpected loss. It can feel confusing, even defeating. "I thought I was past this," you'll think. "Why am I acting like the person I used to be?"

But here's the truth: regression is not failure. It's feedback. It's your system revealing where identity hasn't fully integrated. It's a sign that stress has outpaced your support. That your old wiring—though less dominant—still remembers how to fire. And that the conditions that once shaped you haven't disappeared just because you've decided to evolve. Your nervous system remembers. So does your environment. Your relationships. Your body. That's not weakness. That's human.

The danger isn't in regressing. The danger is in *making it mean something it doesn't*. In telling yourself the old story: "I knew I couldn't change. This is just who I really am." That story is seductive because it offers relief from the tension of becoming. But it is a lie. You *can* change. You *are* changing. The moment you become aware that you've regressed—and choose to return to alignment—you are actively reinforcing Identity 2.0. Not erasing it.

In fact, every regression is an opportunity to upgrade your awareness. To notice: what triggered this? What need wasn't being met? What support system failed me here? What part of me still believes the old identity is safer, easier, or more lovable? You're not just relapsing—you're learning. And if you're willing to pause and listen, regression becomes a teacher. A mirror. A map.

This is why rituals, reflection, and environment matter so deeply. You need scaffolding to support your new self—especially in the moments when life applies pressure. You need ways to return to center, to recalibrate, to remember who you've chosen to become. Without these structures, regression can spiral into shame. With them, it becomes a reminder: this is the work. Not never slipping. But never settling. Never staying in a place that no longer fits.

There's also a subtler form of regression: *success regression*. The paradoxical moment when things finally start going well—and you find yourself self-sabotaging, pulling back, dimming down. Why? Because the old self is uncomfortable with being seen, with being loved, with sustaining joy. It's not used to the new identity *working*. And so it looks for ways to "reset" to what feels familiar. This is why sustainable change must include emotional capacity—not just for struggle, but for fulfillment.

To live as Identity 2.0, you must become someone who notices regression quickly and responds with compassion and course correction—not punishment. You must let go of the idea that your transformation will be tidy. It won't be. But it can be *true*. And truth is stronger than any setback. Strong enough to welcome the returning pattern and say, "I see you. But I don't live there anymore."

Let us now dive into one of the greatest challenges of living in alignment: the tension of evolving in a world that may not evolve with you.

The Inner Circle Challenge

One of the most disorienting parts of identity transformation is not the internal shift—it's the social friction that follows. You've done the work. You've changed the story. You've started showing up as someone new. But the people around you—family, friends, partners, colleagues—don't always adjust. In fact, sometimes they don't even notice. Or worse, they do notice—and they push back. Not always maliciously. Often, they're just confused. "Why are you acting different?" "You've changed." "This isn't like you." And while those words may sound observational, they can land like accusations.

This is the Inner Circle Challenge: how to keep living your truth when the people closest to you are still relating to the person you used to be.

Humans are social creatures. Our identities are not formed in isolation—they're reinforced in relationship. Every role you've played in someone else's life—caretaker, achiever, peacemaker, rebel—has shaped their expectations of you. And when you start acting outside that role, it creates tension. Not just in the relationship, but in your nervous system. Because belonging is a primal need. And stepping into a new identity often threatens the stability of the systems you're embedded in. You're not just changing *your* story. You're disrupting *theirs*.

This is why so many people revert to old patterns—not because they're weak, but because they feel torn between authenticity and acceptance. They ask themselves silently, "Is it worth it?" "Will I lose them if I keep growing?" "Can I belong and evolve at the same time?" These questions are valid. They deserve to be felt. And yet, they must not be allowed to dictate your return to a self that no longer fits.

You must understand: your growth will *always* challenge someone. Not because you're wrong—but because your evolution reflects back to them the places where they've stayed still. Your courage to change may remind them of dreams they abandoned. Your new boundaries may highlight their lack of them. Your healing may shine a light on their avoidance. And if they haven't chosen the path of transformation for themselves, it may feel easier to pull you back than to examine their own discomfort.

This doesn't make them bad people. It makes them human. Most people don't resist your growth because they want to harm you. They resist it because it destabilizes the emotional economy of your connection. If you're no longer playing your old part, who are you to them? What does that mean for their identity? Their role? Their comfort?

So here's the hard truth: not everyone will come with you. Some relationships will stretch. Others will snap. Some people will rise to meet the new version of you. Others will insist on dragging you back to the familiar dance you used to perform. You cannot control their reaction. But you *can* control your choice: to honor the self you're becoming more than the comfort of staying small.

This doesn't mean becoming cold, arrogant, or closed off. It means learning to stay rooted in your new identity *even when others don't understand it yet*. It means having the courage to outgrow relationships that require you to shrink. And it means cultivating connections that support—not sabotage—your becoming.

This is where your courage will be tested most. Not in the solitude of your morning routine, but in the heat of relational dynamics. When your new boundaries are challenged. When your new truth is questioned. When your voice shakes because you're using it in a room where the old you used to stay silent. That's where Identity 2.0 must hold steady. Not with defensiveness, but with quiet conviction. Not with superiority, but with grounded presence.

And here's the beautiful part: as you stay true to your evolution, you'll begin to attract others who are living theirs. New friends. New mentors. New partners. People who don't need you to explain your new self, because they recognize it. They've done the work too. They're not threatened by your light—they're inspired by it. And in their presence, you'll exhale. You'll remember: you are not alone in this becoming.

Now, let's discuss how to keep your identity from becoming rigid or performative—how to treat it as a *living system* that grows with you.

Identity 2.0 as a Living System

Most people think of identity as something you find, or decide, or declare. But if your identity is to remain alive—if it's to evolve with your life rather than calcify into another cage—it must become something else entirely: a living system. Not a frozen self-image or carefully managed persona, but a dynamic, adaptive way of being that grows as you grow. Like any living system, it requires nourishment, feedback, and space to breathe.

The moment you declare your Identity 2.0, your nervous system begins adapting. But so does your environment, your language, your habits, and your relationships. Identity is not static—it's emergent. It reveals more of itself the more you live it. What felt like a brave stretch two months ago may now feel like second nature. What once felt misaligned may no longer even tempt you. And yet, the work isn't done. Because the moment you treat your identity as complete, you risk mistaking comfort for truth.

A living identity doesn't resist refinement—it *requires* it. Not because you're chasing some idealized self, but because you're staying present to what life is asking of you next. You notice the edges where growth is needed. You listen to the whispers of discomfort that say, "Something here no longer fits." You pay attention when joy starts to drain, when resentment creeps in, when a once-exciting path starts to feel mechanical. These are not signs of failure. They are signs of evolution.

To hold your identity as a living system means releasing the illusion that you'll ever be "finished." There is no final version of you—only deeper congruence. You are not a product to perfect. You are a process to participate in. And that participation is what keeps you alive, awake, and aligned.

This also means resisting the temptation to turn your new identity into another performance. Especially if it's brought you some success. It's easy to begin curating your transformation, showcasing only the most polished parts, pretending the struggle has ended. But that rigidity suffocates authenticity. Your identity is not a brand. It's a *relationship*—between your inner truth and the outer world. When it becomes performative, you lose access to your own becoming.

Living as Identity 2.0 means embracing humility. Staying open to change. Being willing to reexamine what used to work. You may outgrow strategies that once saved you. You may be called to take risks that feel inconvenient. You may realize that the person you've become is capable of more honesty, more impact, or more softness than you previously allowed. This is the grace of holding your identity loosely—not because you're unsure, but because you're *awake*.

A living identity also means developing a long-term relationship with *integrity*. The commitment to stay internally aligned—even when external circumstances shift. Even when others don't agree. Even when your goals evolve. Your identity must be flexible enough to grow and firm enough to guide. Like the roots of a tree—anchored, yet responsive to the seasons.

The more you treat your identity as a living system, the less fragile it becomes. You won't panic when things fall apart, because you know how to rebuild. You won't cling to roles that no longer serve, because you've practiced letting go. You won't fear change, because you've become a participant in your own evolution.

And when others see you—really see you—they'll sense something rare: not just someone who has changed, but someone who is *still changing*. Someone who is not trapped by their past, nor obsessed with their image. Someone who lives with a kind of fluid strength—a strength rooted not in certainty, but in *congruence*.

Before we move into the final chapter, let's bring it all down to earth. We'll explore the rituals, rhythms, and seasonal recalibrations that help keep Identity 2.0 alive—not just as a concept, but as a lived experience.

Designing a Ritual Life

To live as Identity 2.0 is to understand that your life is not just something to manage—it's something to *honor*. Not through occasional breakthroughs, but through *daily devotion*. Ritual is how you translate the sacred into the practical. It's how you reinforce who you are becoming—not with fanfare, but with rhythm. It's how you root transformation into the structure of your life so that it endures beyond the emotional high of insight.

Rituals are not routines. Routines are what you do to stay organized. Rituals are what you do to stay *aligned*. A ritual doesn't have to be elaborate. It doesn't need incense or silence or ceremony (though it might include those). What matters is *intention*. You wake up and speak your identity out loud—not as an affirmation, but as a reminder: "This is who I am now." You journal—not to vent, but to track congruence. You move your body—not just to stay fit, but to stay *present*. You enter your workday with a pause, a breath, a grounding phrase that connects action to purpose. These micro-moments matter. They are the anchors of identity.

In a culture obsessed with novelty, ritual gives your nervous system something to rely on. Something steady. Something sacred. It turns your home into a place that reflects your values. It turns your morning coffee into a meditation. It turns your calendar into a mirror of what matters. It reclaims your attention from the chaos of the external world and brings it back to the internal compass you've spent this entire journey uncovering.

But rituals aren't just for the ordinary days. They are essential during transitions. Birthdays. Anniversaries. Job changes. Relationship shifts. Setbacks. Victories. These are not just events—they are identity thresholds. And without ritual, they pass unmarked. You move on without integrating what they meant. A ritual is how you pause to *process,* to recalibrate, to let go of who you were and make space for who you're becoming. Even something as simple as writing a letter to your past self—or lighting a candle for the future you're stepping into—can create an emotional bridge between identities.

You can also design *seasonal* rituals. A quarterly check-in where you revisit your Identity 2.0 declaration. A digital detox every few months to reset your nervous system. A monthly dinner with people who speak to your highest self. These aren't luxuries. They are necessities. Because the world is constantly pulling you back toward fragmentation, toward performance, toward old roles. Ritual is your resistance. Ritual is your return.

And perhaps most powerfully, ritual gives you a sense of authorship. You stop waiting for life to hand you meaning and begin generating it. You become the one who decides what's worth honoring, what's worth remembering, what's worth repeating. Your days are no longer just tasks to complete, but vessels for becoming.

This is how Identity 2.0 lives—not as a concept, not as a peak experience, but as a rhythm. A steady pulse beneath the noise. A quiet contract between who you were and who you refuse to stop becoming. And over time, those rituals—those small, sacred repetitions—become your life's fingerprint. Not because they make you successful in the eyes of the world, but because they make you *true* in the eyes of yourself.

In the final chapter, we'll gather everything you've learned. And we'll turn it into a system. A blueprint. A way to engineer your identity in alignment with the life you most deeply desire to live.

> "Life isn't about finding yourself. Life is about creating yourself."
>
> —George Bernard Shaw

"The goal isn't to become someone new once. It's to keep becoming - uncovering more of yourself in the process."

-Keith Leonard

CHAPTER 10
Engineering Your Identity

Lasting change flows from the top down. Purpose leads. Identity aligns. Everything else follows.

Becoming the Engineer of Who You Are

After all you've uncovered in this book—after the peeling back, the truth-telling, the awakening—it's time to do more than understand identity. It's time to **build it.** This final chapter is not another reflection point. It's a **construction site** for your future self. A place where philosophy becomes architecture, where clarity becomes structure, and where the life you envision becomes a system you live.

Because here's the reality most people miss: real transformation doesn't begin with behavior. It doesn't start with new habits or better routines or more discipline. **It begins with a shift in who you believe you are**—and why you're here. Purpose and identity form the blueprint. They set the structure. Once those are clear and alive within you, change becomes less of a struggle and more of a flow. Everything else—your beliefs, your skills, your actions, even your environment—*adjusts downward* to meet the new you.

This is the fatal flaw in most personal growth strategies: they try to start at the bottom. Change your space. Change your habits. Then maybe you'll feel different. But you won't. Because the core programming—the "you" running the show—hasn't been updated. You're still operating from the same identity, just trying harder. It's like installing new apps on an outdated operating system. Eventually, they crash.

But when you start from the top—from *who you are becoming* and *why it matters*—you give the rest of your life something solid to reorient around. That's what this chapter is about: not inspiration, not motivation, but **identity engineering**. The deliberate, structured act of designing your self-concept from the top down—and reinforcing it at every level of your life.

You don't need to wait to become this person. You *decide*—and then you *build*. You engineer a new internal architecture that governs how you show up, how you think, how you grow, and what you tolerate. And because you've done the deep work of this book, your new identity won't be a fantasy or a mask. It will be a **return to who you were always capable of becoming.**

Below are the 10 steps to engineering Identity 2.0. These steps move top-down, from the deepest layers of meaning and identity into the outer layers of action, habit, and design. Follow them in sequence, and you will build a life that not only reflects your transformation—but *reinforces it every single day.*

THE 10 STEPS TO ENGINEERING YOUR IDENTITY

1. **Define Your Identity 2.0 Declaration**
   Craft a bold and specific identity statement that describes the version of you that you are choosing to become. Not a wish list—an embodiment.

2. **Clarify Your Core Purpose**
   Uncover the reason beneath your reinvention. Name the deeper "why" that gives your identity gravity, direction, and meaning.

3. **Upgrade Your Belief System**
   Audit and rewire the internal rules that govern your behavior. Replace inherited or limiting beliefs with empowered, aligned convictions.

4. **Create Your Capability Map**
   Design a deliberate learning and development strategy that supports your new identity and fuels long-term confidence.

5. **Anchor New Behaviors in Identity**
   Move beyond habit tracking to identity-based action. Align your daily behaviors with who you've declared yourself to be.

6. **Rehearse Identity Through Language and Imagery**
   Leverage visualization, self-talk, and symbolic anchoring to make your identity emotionally and neurologically real.

7. **Align Relationships with Your Future Self**
   Upgrade or redefine social dynamics to support the new you. Navigate conversations, boundaries, and influence with clarity.

8. **Design Environments that Reflect Your Identity**
   Curate spaces—physical, digital, and energetic—that echo and reinforce your chosen self.

9. **Create Rituals for Daily and Seasonal Reinforcement**
   Build rhythms that maintain identity alignment through repetition, reflection, and recommitment.

10. **Establish Your Recoding Cycle**
    Engineer a system for ongoing recalibration. Learn how to evolve Identity 2.0 into 3.0 and beyond as your life expands.

This is the chapter where your transformation becomes structural. Until now, you've been reflecting, uncovering, and awakening to what's possible. But this chapter isn't just for reading — it's for *building*. This is where insight turns into engineering. Where the abstract becomes tangible.

You are not waiting for life to hand you a new self. You're ready to *construct* it. Step by step. Layer by layer. From the top down, or the bottom up — depending on what this season of your life demands.

Use this chapter as a tool. Write in it. Highlight it. Doodle in the margins. Draw maps, scribble notes, sketch diagrams of the future you're stepping into. Make it messy if you need to — this isn't a chapter to keep pristine, it's a chapter to *own*.

This is your personal blueprint for Identity 2.0. The more you engage with it, the more real it becomes. Your next self isn't waiting on clarity — it's waiting on *commitment*.

So don't hold back. Treat these pages like a workshop. A design lab. A canvas.

Every answer you write, every question you pause with, every intention you clarify — it all becomes part of the architecture of who you are becoming.

Let's build it. Together. Boldly. Intentionally. And on purpose.

STEP ONE

Your Identity 2.0 Declaration

You are not discovering who you are. You are deciding who you will be – and proving it with your life.

At some point in your life, you stopped asking the question, "Who do I want to become?" and started asking, "What do people expect of me?" That shift was subtle, and it likely happened early. You took on roles, identities, and labels—not because they were chosen, but because they were *rewarded*. You became the high achiever, the helper, the quiet one, the reliable one, the rebel, the peacemaker. You inherited a self-image based on approval, survival, and pattern. And somewhere along the way, you confused that constructed identity with your truth.

But now, standing here in the final chapter, you know something different: **you are not fixed. You are not final. You are not a product of your past.** You are the author. And the act of engineering your life begins with a conscious, deliberate redefinition of *who you are*. Not in vague affirmations or temporary mood swings—but in a living, breathing declaration of identity. A commitment to becoming.

Your Identity 2.0 Declaration is not a personality test. It's not a list of traits. It's a conscious articulation of the person you choose to embody—at your best, under pressure, and in motion. It's a design blueprint that you will reinforce at every level of your life. And the power of this declaration lies not in how loud it is, but in how true it feels.

To write your declaration, begin by answering five powerful prompts. These will help you move from abstract intentions to embodied identity:

Who am I becoming?
Describe this future version of yourself as if it is already real. Use present-tense language. Not "I want to be more confident," but "I am someone who trusts their voice, owns their presence, and speaks with clarity and purpose."

What do I believe that reinforces this version of me?
List the beliefs that this identity holds as truth. These might sound like: "Discomfort is a sign of growth," or "I create value everywhere I go," or "I am responsible for my energy and impact."

What am I capable of as this identity?
Name the skills, attitudes, and internal resources that support your identity. Think of this as the toolbox you're building—not because you've mastered everything yet, but because this is who you are committed to becoming.

How do I behave when I live from this identity?
Define how this version of you acts—under pressure, in relationships, during uncertainty, at the start of the day. Be specific. What do you *do* differently? What do you no longer tolerate?

Why does this version of me matter?
This is your personal anchor. Your "why." When growth gets uncomfortable—and it will—this answer will pull you forward. Is it to become a better parent? To live aligned with your values? To heal a generational wound? To fulfill your potential with dignity? Make it count.

Once you've answered these, craft a single paragraph—your Identity 2.0 Declaration. Something you can read aloud each morning. Something that feels too big for who you were, but just right for who you're becoming. Something like these:

"I am a powerful, grounded, and courageous leader. I tell the truth with clarity and compassion. I am calm under pressure and centered in purpose. I value presence over perfection and impact over approval. I act boldly and think long-term. I choose growth over comfort and service over ego. I know who I am, and I walk into every room as that person—no matter who's watching."

"I am a visionary creator and a disciplined artist. I bring ideas to life with focus, fire, and joy. I trust my instincts and take action even when I feel fear. I am not here to fit in—I'm here to express what only I can. I follow through. I finish what I start. I turn inspiration into impact and imagination into income. I honor my gifts by using them fully. I don't wait for permission. I create the path. Every project I touch reflects the clarity of who I've chosen to become."

"I am a bold, visionary entrepreneur. I take calculated risks with courage and resilience. I don't chase trends—I create value. I trust my instincts and back them with action. I lead with integrity, build with purpose, and scale with intention. I prioritize people over ego and long-term impact over short-term gain. When I hit resistance, I get resourceful. I see challenges as invitations to grow. I own my time, my vision, and my voice. I don't just build a business—I build a legacy."

Your version will be different. It should be. This isn't a slogan. It's a code. And it should feel *alive*. You should feel slightly uncomfortable saying it at first—not because it's fake, but because it demands something real from you. That tension? That's the edge of your current identity. That's where the shift begins.

Create your Identity 2.0 Declaration here:

Your Identity 2.0 Declaration is not a one-time exercise. It's a *living statement*—something you'll revisit, refine, and reinforce. Speak it. Post it. Practice it. Make decisions from it. Because your brain believes what you prove. And the more you act in alignment with this declaration, the more your nervous system will adopt it as truth.

This is not about becoming someone *else*. It's about removing the layers that never belonged, and stepping fully into the self you were meant to lead with. The self you must now *build* around.

In step two, we'll go deeper into the "why." You'll connect this new identity to the **core purpose** that gives it gravity and direction—because purpose is what makes identity sustainable.

STEP TWO

Clarify Your Core Purpose

Identity without purpose is directionless. Purpose gives your new self something to serve— something to live for.

Now that you've defined who you are becoming, you must decide why it matters. Not just to you, but to something larger. Because when change is fueled by vanity, ego, or surface-level goals, it burns out fast. But when change is rooted in **purpose**, it becomes inexhaustible. Purpose is the emotional engine behind identity. It's what gives your transformation weight, direction, and meaning—especially when motivation fades and discomfort rises.

Most people drift through life asking questions like, "What should I do next?" or "What's my passion?" But those are the wrong questions. Purpose doesn't show up in the form of a job title or a single cause. Purpose begins with a deeper, more confronting inquiry: **What am I here to give?** What is the impact I want my life to have? Who will suffer if I shrink back into the old version of me? What part of the world needs what I've been too afraid to bring forward?

These are not small questions. They are identity-altering. And that's the point. Purpose is not a Pinterest quote—it's a **summons.** It calls you out of your smallness. It asks you to do the emotional heavy lifting of alignment. It invites you to build a life that is not just functional or impressive, but *true*.

When you begin to live from Identity 2.0, you will feel a gravitational pull toward contribution. You'll crave a form of expression that isn't just about your success, but about your significance. You'll begin to feel the difference between achievement and *alignment*. And you'll start to recognize that your new identity is not here to serve your comfort—it's here to serve a cause.

So how do you find that cause? Start by reflecting on these questions:

What injustice or dysfunction makes you angry, sad, or restless?

What problem in the world—or in your community—feels personal to you, even if you're not directly affected?

What have you suffered through, overcome, or survived?

What wound have you earned the wisdom to help heal in others?

What kind of impact would break your heart not to make?

If your time here ended next year, what would you regret not saying, building, sharing, or becoming?

Who are the people you feel called to serve, uplift, or empower?

Are they your children? Your clients? Young women? Aging parents? Aspiring creators? Struggling leaders?

What feels sacred to you, even if it's not popular or profitable?

What value, principle, or vision feels like a thread that runs through everything you do?

Your answers will begin to form a throughline—a kind of spiritual backbone that can support the weight of your evolving identity. That's your purpose. It doesn't need to be eloquent or dramatic. It just needs to feel *real*. Something like:

"I exist to empower people to trust their voice."

"My life is meant to restore dignity to those who've lost it."

"I help others rise by becoming the version of myself I once needed."

"I create spaces where healing and truth can coexist."

"I wake people up to their own potential."

Once you've named your purpose—even in rough form—it becomes the *anchor* of everything that follows. Your beliefs will align with it. Your skills will grow to meet it. Your actions will reflect it. And your environment will begin to serve it.

This is the beauty of engineering from the top down: every layer becomes *easier to change* once you know what you're changing *for*.

When identity is aligned with purpose, you stop chasing outcomes. You stop measuring your life by metrics alone.

You start to feel a deep kind of clarity—not about what you do, but about *who you are when you're doing it*.

And that kind of congruence can carry you through anything.

In the next step, we'll address the beliefs that either support or sabotage that congruence—and teach you how to upgrade your internal rulebook to match your new identity and purpose.

STEP THREE

Upgrade Your Belief System

Your life can only grow as wide and high as your beliefs allow. Upgrade the ceiling – and the structure expands.

Every human being lives within a set of invisible rules—beliefs so deeply embedded they don't feel like beliefs. They feel like *truth*. You don't wake up in the morning and remind yourself, "Gravity exists." You just operate as if it does. The same is true with your identity beliefs. Somewhere along the way, you internalized quiet conclusions about who you are, what you deserve, how far you can go, and what is or isn't possible for someone "like you." These beliefs weren't always spoken aloud. Often, they were shaped by repetition, pain, rejection, or reward. But make no mistake: they're governing you.

To fully embody Identity 2.0, you must take your beliefs off autopilot. You must become conscious of the quiet laws you've been living under and deliberately rewrite the ones that keep your life smaller than your vision. Because beliefs are not passive. They don't just sit there. They *filter everything*. They shape how you interpret feedback, how you handle failure, how you navigate risk, how you love, how you lead, and how you self-sabotage. If you try to build a new identity while dragging old beliefs with you, you'll stall every time. Your nervous system won't allow you to outgrow your perceived truth.

So the first step in this upgrade is awareness. Get brutally honest about the beliefs that are still operating in the background. Ask yourself:

"What do I believe about people like me?"

"What do I believe about success, safety, money, love, limits, or leadership?"

"What beliefs did I absorb from my family, culture, religion, or early education?"

"Which ones do I hear myself repeat in moments of stress or decision?"

Write them down. All of them. Even the ones that feel irrational. Especially the ones that feel inherited. You may uncover beliefs like:

"I'm just not good at that."
"People will leave if I change too much."
"If I'm not the best, I'll be forgotten."
"I have to do everything myself."
"I don't deserve more than what I have."

Once these limiting beliefs are named, you can begin to dismantle them. One powerful method is to interrogate them with the same clarity you would use if someone else said them to your face. Ask:

"Who taught me this?"
"Is this belief always true?"
"What has it cost me to believe this?"
"What would my life look like if I couldn't believe this anymore?"
"What new belief would serve my Identity 2.0?"

This is not about positive thinking. It's about *accurate alignment*. An upgraded belief is not just more inspiring—it's more *useful*. It helps you take better action. It reduces internal resistance. It gives you permission to expand. For example, "I'm not a disciplined person" becomes "I'm someone who creates structure to honor my purpose." "I'm not creative" becomes "I'm learning how to express my voice in new ways." "People always leave" becomes "I now choose relationships where mutual growth is welcome."

Once you've identified and rewritten key beliefs, you must reinforce them. Beliefs don't stick because you *decide* them—they stick because you *prove* them. This is where the rest of your Identity 2.0 architecture matters. When your actions, environments, and rituals support your new beliefs, your nervous system starts to accept them. You become someone who doesn't just say, "I am capable"—you start doing things capable people do. The proof rewires the program.

Remember: your beliefs are not reflections of reality. They're *filters* for it. Change the filter, and your entire experience of life changes with it. That's not magic. That's psychology. And that's why this step is so critical. Because until you consciously upgrade your beliefs, you'll unconsciously recreate the same identity—even inside a new vision.

Now that your identity and purpose have been declared—and your beliefs aligned—it's time to equip yourself with the skills that will turn intention into capacity. In the next step, you'll build a Capability Map to identify, develop, and embody the strengths required to live as your future self.

STEP FOUR

Create Your Capability Map

You don't need to become someone else. You need to build the skills that allow your future self to come alive.

One of the most damaging illusions in personal growth is that people who are living the life you want are somehow "naturally" talented. That they were born confident. That they just "have it." That they always knew what they were doing. But identity isn't a talent. It's not encoded in your DNA. It's constructed—through repetition, reinforcement, and *capability*. And behind every version of you that seems just out of reach is a set of skills you haven't yet developed.

That's why you must stop treating capability like personality. You're not "bad with people." You're not "just not good at business." You're not "terrible at discipline." Those are not traits—they're temporary skill gaps that can be filled. But only if you recognize them as such. When you frame a limitation as a fixed part of who you are, you seal it in place. When you frame it as a capability you're willing to build, it becomes a doorway into your next level.

This is where your Capability Map comes in. It's a tool for naming, organizing, and intentionally developing the abilities that match your Identity 2.0. Not based on what you've done in the past, but based on who you've decided to become. The question is no longer "What am I good at?" It's "What does the version of me I'm becoming *know how to do*—and how do I begin learning that?"

Start by revisiting your Identity 2.0 Declaration. Read it slowly. Picture yourself living it out fully. Then ask:

"What skills would I need to become this version of me, consistently?"

"What emotional capacities would I need to

strengthen?"

"What leadership, communication, creative, or practical abilities would I need to build or refine?"

"Where do I feel underdeveloped, insecure, or stuck—and what specific capability would resolve that?"

For example, if your Identity 2.0 includes becoming a calm, confident leader, your Capability Map might include:

Emotional regulation under pressure
Public speaking or facilitation
Conflict navigation and difficult conversations
Strategic delegation
Boundary setting and time ownership

If your new identity involves becoming a creator, healer, or mentor, your capability list might include:

Deep listening and empathy
Structured thinking and planning
Storytelling or teaching
Visibility and self-expression
Managing your energy and creative rhythms

Once you've mapped the core capabilities, prioritize them. What's most essential to develop first? What would have the most immediate impact on your identity embodiment? Choose one or two to begin with. Then, for each, define a simple Learning Plan. This could include:

A book or course to complete
A mentor to reach out to
A project or challenge to initiate

A skill-practice ritual (daily journaling, weekly role-play, coaching sessions)
Metrics or milestones to track growth

Sample Map for my ID 2.0 (Bold Entrepreneur)

Capability	Learning Plan	Priority
Investing	Study 3 Investment Strategies	1
Emotional Intel.	Read Daniel Goleman's work	2
Public Speaking	Take a course / Watch speeches	3
Time Mgmt	Read "Time Management Magic" by Lee Cockerell	4

Don't over-engineer this. You're not trying to master everything in a month. You're choosing to *invest in becoming*. You're demonstrating to your nervous system, your belief system, and your future self: "I am willing to do the work that this identity requires." And that willingness is what sets Identity 2.0 apart from fantasy.

You're not just imagining a better you—you're building the muscle to live it.

Understand this: you don't need to be fully capable before you show up as your new identity. But you do need to be in motion.

Confidence is not the result of already having the skill. It's the result of proving to yourself that you're becoming the kind of person who acquires it.

Now it's time to create your map:

Capability	Learning Plan	Priority

This Capability Map is not just a plan. It's a contract. It says, "I will not let my old limits define my future." It says, "If I don't know how yet, I'll learn." It says, "My potential is not optional—it's a responsibility I'm finally accepting."

Now that you've named the capabilities that empower your new identity, it's time to translate that into *daily behavior*—not as performance, but as practice. In the next step, you'll learn how to anchor your actions in identity, so that every choice you make becomes another thread in the fabric of who you are becoming.

STEP FIVE

Anchor New Behaviors in Identity

You don't become a new version of yourself by thinking differently. You become it by behaving like it already matters.

Every change you've made so far has reshaped the *internal scaffolding* of your identity—who you believe yourself to be, what you stand for, and what you're building toward. But none of that becomes real unless it's *embodied*. Your identity isn't defined by what you say you value—it's defined by the decisions you make when no one's watching. That's why the next phase of your transformation requires you to bring identity into your everyday behavior.

Most people try to build new habits the wrong way. They focus on willpower or rewards. They track streaks. They set alarms and hope for the best. But these methods often fail because they're behavior-first. If the underlying identity hasn't changed, the nervous system rejects the new action like a virus. It feels fake. It doesn't "belong." Sooner or later, your old self reclaims control. Not because you're lazy or broken, but because you never taught your brain who you were becoming.

The solution is not to *force* new behavior. It's to *anchor* it to your identity. That means choosing actions not just because they're good for you, but because they *reinforce the person you've decided to be*. You start behaving *from* identity, not *toward* it.

Here's how to do it.

First, identify keystone behaviors that are aligned with your Identity 2.0 Declaration. These are small, repeatable actions that feel like signatures of your new self. For example:

The version of you who is calm and grounded meditates for five minutes before responding to tension.

The version of you who is confident and creative shares your ideas before they're perfect.

The version of you who is self-respecting turns off the laptop at 6:00 p.m.

The version of you who is a powerful communicator asks for what they want, clearly and directly.

The version of you who is purpose-driven speaks up in meetings—even when it's uncomfortable.

The key here is to go beyond productivity hacks. Don't pick behaviors that simply make you "better." Pick the ones that make you feel more *yourself*. These are identity-building behaviors. They're not just tools—they're *declarations in motion*.

Next, create a repetition strategy. Identity change doesn't come from a single act of courage. It comes from *consistent reinforcement*. That means:

Choose one or two identity-aligned behaviors and repeat them daily.

Track not the result, but the *alignment*. Did I act like the version of me I've declared?

Celebrate each repetition—not for perfection, but for integrity. Each time you behave as your Identity 2.0, your nervous system takes note: "This is who we are now."

It also helps to create behavioral triggers—built-in cues that prompt identity action. For example:

"When I feel anxious, I respond by breathing and remembering my purpose."

"When I step into a room, I lead with presence, not apology."

"When I start my day, I review my Identity 2.0 statement before checking email."

These triggers turn intention into automatic response. They rewire the pathways that once defaulted to fear, avoidance, or self-doubt. They become rituals of alignment—not effortful, but *naturalized.*

And if you miss a day? You don't start over. You remember who you are. You don't break the identity—you *reclaim it.*

Every stumble is just a test of whether the new identity has roots. Forgive the lapse. Reaffirm the vision. Move forward without drama.

Here's what's most important: behavior is not a performance. It's a conversation between you and your future.

Every time you behave as your next-level self, you are saying: "I belong there." You're collapsing the gap between who you were and who you're becoming—not by pretending, but by *participating in the becoming.*

Now, identify your keystone behaviors and create a repetition strategy for each one:

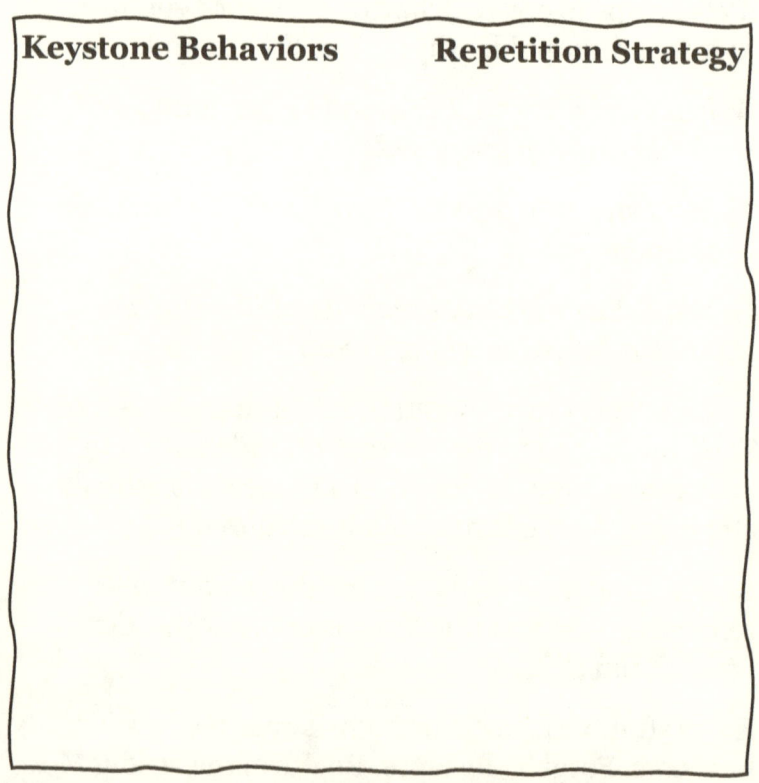

In the next step, you'll build the environments that make these behaviors easier, more natural, and more consistent—so that your surroundings no longer pull you backward, but propel you forward.

STEP SIX

Redesign Your Environment to Reflect Your Identity 2.0

Your environment is not neutral. It is either reinforcing the old you – or inviting the new one forward.

Most people don't realize how much of their behavior is shaped by what surrounds them. You can have the clearest identity, the deepest purpose, the most empowering beliefs—but if you're still living inside the physical, social, and digital environments built for your old self, you will be quietly pulled back into your past. Your environment is not just a setting. It's a *mirror*. It reflects and reinforces who you believe yourself to be. And until you update that reflection, your transformation will feel like trying to breathe new air in an old room.

That's why Identity 2.0 requires a conscious act of environmental design. This doesn't mean throwing out your furniture or quitting your job tomorrow. It means looking at every part of your physical, relational, and digital world and asking: *Does this align with the version of me I've chosen to become?* If not, it needs to change—not because it's "bad," but because it's outdated. The wardrobe of your old life doesn't fit the future you. It's time to renovate the stage so the new performance can begin.

Start with your physical space. Walk through your home, your car, your workspace. Observe with new eyes. What part of this space feels like your future? What feels like your past? Look at your desk—is it organized in a way that supports clarity and focus? Open your closet—does it reflect how you want to show up in the world? Look at your kitchen, your nightstand, your bookshelves, even the art on your walls—are these expressions of the life you're stepping into or remnants of the one you're leaving behind?

You don't need to redecorate your entire life. Small, symbolic changes are often the most powerful. Create a morning ritual space with a candle and journal. Move your exercise gear into plain view. Place your Identity 2.0 statement on your bathroom mirror. Replace clutter with clarity. Each change is a vote for who you're becoming.

Next, consider your digital environment. Your phone and laptop are not just tools—they're *portals*. And most people let them become cluttered, chaotic extensions of the very identity they're trying to shed.

Unfollow voices that trigger insecurity or self-doubt.

Mute the notifications that disrupt your presence.

Curate your feed to reflect the content that uplifts, educates, or reinforces your new values.

Organize your files, clean up your bookmarks, create folders that mirror your future focus—not your old overwhelm.

Make your digital life a place your Identity 2.0 would want to live in.

Then there's the social environment. This is often the hardest to change, but also the most critical. People are mirrors. Some will reflect your growth. Others will try to reflect your past, because it's more comfortable for them. You don't have to cut everyone out of your life. But you do need to audit your inner circle.

Who challenges you to rise?

Who anchors you in your old patterns?

Who sees your potential?

Who secretly benefits from your playing small?

Upgrade your environment by upgrading your conversations. Speak from your new identity, even if it feels awkward. Share your purpose and your vision out loud. Invite people into your growth—and observe who cheers you on, and who becomes silent. You'll know what to do.

Finally, create identity-aligned zones. Design spaces and routines that trigger the future version of you. A writing corner. A meditation cushion. A Sunday prep ritual. A Wednesday night creative block. These are not just tasks—they are *temples*. Places where your future self shows up reliably and begins to feel at home.

When you redesign your environment, you're not just moving objects. You're moving energy. You're signaling to your brain, your body, and your unconscious: *This is who I am now. This is how we live now.*

And in doing so, you reduce the friction of change. You stop trying to force your new identity into a context built for someone else—and instead, you build a world that matches the future you're already stepping into.

In the next step, you'll go even deeper—integrating these changes through rituals, repetition, and relationship. Because identity doesn't stick because you changed. It sticks because you *stayed*.

Sketch out your environmental upgrades here:

STEP SEVEN

Reinforce Identity through Ritual and Repetition

Change doesn't last because it's dramatic. It lasts because it's remembered — again, and again, and again.

If your identity is the software, and your behaviors are the code it runs, then repetition is the installation process. Nothing becomes natural, effortless, or deeply integrated until it has been lived enough times to become *normal*. And while the world celebrates sudden breakthroughs, transformation isn't about what happens in a weekend—it's about what happens every morning, every choice, every week, every conversation, until the new self becomes as familiar as the old one used to be.

This is why ritual matters. Repetition is not just about discipline. It's about *identity maintenance.*

Your brain is a pattern recognition machine. It will believe what you prove. And the more consistently you live in alignment with your Identity 2.0—through thought, behavior, language, and presence—the more it becomes who you are. Not through rigid routines, but by deliberate consistency.

You're not trying to impress the world. You're teaching yourself who you've become.

Start by creating daily identity rituals. These aren't long, complicated practices. They are brief, intentional acts that begin and end your day with a reminder: *This is who I am now.* Examples include:

Reading your Identity 2.0 statement aloud in the morning

Writing a single sentence in your journal: "Today, I'll show up as..."

Doing a 5-minute embodiment practice (movement, breath, visualization) to step into your chosen identity

Asking one powerful question at night: "Did I live aligned today?"

These are not chores. They are *check-ins*. They remind you that you are not reacting to life—you are creating yourself inside of it.

Then build weekly reflection rituals. Once a week, pause and assess. Not to criticize yourself, but to witness your evolution. Ask:

What aligned behaviors did I live this week?

Where did I revert to my old identity—and why?

What did I learn about myself through this week's challenges?

What do I want to reinforce, remove, or recommit to in the week ahead?

These reflections turn setbacks into strategy and wins into anchors. You stop living on autopilot and start living on intention.

Capture your daily Identity 2.0 rituals:

Now capture your reflection rituals:

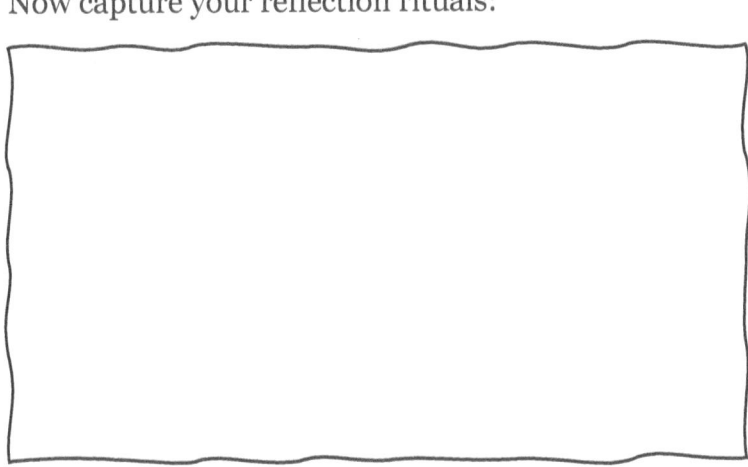

Next, use identity triggers throughout your day. Place small cues in your environment that remind you who you are becoming. A bracelet. A wallpaper on your phone. A single word taped to your laptop. A note on your mirror.

These are not trinkets—they are *symbols*. They speak directly to your unconscious and re-center you when life gets noisy.

And when it comes to repetition, remember: ritual beats willpower. You don't have to feel like your future self to act like them. You act like them—reliably, repeatedly—and the feeling *catches up*. Emotion follows action. Confidence follows consistency.

But identity also needs relational reinforcement. That's where your community, your conversations, and your social contracts come into play. If you keep repeating old stories with old people in old roles, your new self won't stick.

That's why we'll turn next to the relationships in your life—and how to align them with who you're becoming.

Because the most powerful repetition doesn't come from solo work. It comes from the people who mirror back your future until it feels like your present.

STEP EIGHT

Align Your Relationships with Your Identity

You can't become a new version of yourself while performing your old role in someone else's story.

Nothing will test your identity transformation more than your relationships. People aren't just people—they are emotional gravity wells that pull you into old patterns, roles, and reflexes. You could do every exercise in this book, rewire your beliefs, rebuild your behaviors, and redesign your environment—but if you're still surrounded by people who treat you like the version of you you've outgrown, your nervous system will struggle to fully step forward. Why? Because identity isn't just internal. It's *relational*. It lives not just in your own mind, but in the reflected expectations of the people closest to you.

Many of the roles we perform—"the strong one," "the fixer," "the quiet one," "the one who never complains"—weren't chosen. They were inherited. We were assigned these parts by families, friends, partners, or teams who needed us to show up in a specific way to keep the system stable. And often, we complied. Not because it was who we were, but because it was safer than disrupting the script.

But now, you're writing a new script. And it will require difficult choices, honest conversations, and courageous boundaries. Not everyone in your life will understand your change. Some will resist it. Some will feel threatened by it. Some will pretend to support it but subtly sabotage your growth with guilt, silence, or sarcasm. This doesn't make them bad people. It just means they are mirrors of your past—and your reflection is shifting faster than they're comfortable with.

This is why it's time to audit your relationships through the lens of Identity 2.0. Begin by asking:

Who truly sees the version of me I'm becoming?

Who celebrates my growth instead of tolerating it?

Who triggers my regressions, even unintentionally?

Who do I feel most like myself around—and who do I feel like I'm performing for?

You don't have to burn bridges. You don't have to cut people out of your life. But you *do* have to get honest about the energetic cost of staying enmeshed in dynamics that reinforce your old identity. You can love someone and still create distance.

You can respect someone and still outgrow the way they relate to you. You are allowed to change, even if it makes others uncomfortable.

Next, update your social contracts. These are the invisible agreements that govern your interactions: the roles you play, the things you never say, the emotional labor you silently carry.

Many of these contracts were formed unconsciously. Now, it's time to renegotiate them with intention. That might mean:

Having a conversation where you share what's shifting inside you.

Asking for different kinds of support.

Saying no to expectations that no longer serve your identity.

Allowing relationships to recalibrate—or even dissolve—so that you can breathe.

And just as important as making space is filling it with alignment. Seek out relationships that reflect your values and reinforce your new self. Join a group, community, or circle where your future is not only welcomed—but expected. Surround yourself with people who speak the language of growth, who normalize transformation, and who hold you accountable to your higher standard.

How will you audit and adjust your relationships to align with your Identity 2.0?

No identity sticks in isolation. We become who we spend time with. We rise or shrink to match the emotional tone of our relationships. And when you are consistently seen as the version of you that you are choosing—not the one you inherited—that reflection becomes a powerful ally in your integration.

The next step will show you how to *cement* this identity across time: through rituals, seasons, and systems of reflection that ensure you're not just stepping into your future—but *staying there*.

STEP NINE

Design a System for Ongoing Reinvention

You are not a final product. You are a living system. And every season of life will require a different version of you.

Transformation is not a one-time event. It's not something you do once, check off, and coast on forever. Identity—true identity—is not a static label. It's an evolving ecosystem. The version of you that fits this season may not fit the next. And that's not failure. That's nature. Just as trees shed their leaves to conserve energy and prepare for new growth, your identity will need periodic pruning, refreshing, and reimagining. This is not something to resist—it's something to design for.

That's why sustainable transformation requires a reinvention system—a rhythm of self-reflection and recalibration that keeps you aligned with your deeper purpose even as the external world shifts. Without this, even the most profound breakthroughs fade. Life changes, but you don't adapt. And soon, your identity becomes outdated once again—not because you weren't committed, but because you didn't have a system for evolving on purpose.

Begin by creating seasonal identity check-ins. These are quarterly or biannual moments where you step back from the day-to-day and ask: *Who am I becoming now?* This isn't just about setting goals—it's about assessing alignment. Use questions like:

What parts of my Identity 2.0 still feel alive and empowering?

What aspects feel heavy, outdated, or performative?

What am I being called to expand into that wasn't visible before?

What's no longer working—and what's ready to emerge?

Let these reflections inform micro-adjustments to your Identity Declaration. Add, refine, or release language based on what feels *true* now—not just aspirational.

When will you audit your identity for alignment? And what questions will you ask?

Next, design identity rituals around life transitions. Whenever you end or begin something significant—a job, a relationship, a move, a birthday—create space for an intentional review. Ask:

Who was I in that last chapter?

What did I learn, grieve, or gain?

What identity must I let go of to fully step into what's next?

Mark the moment. Write a letter to your former self. Burn an old journal. Take a solo walk. Do something *symbolic* to honor the transition.

Ritual helps your nervous system understand: the chapter is complete—and a new self is welcome here.

Also, build feedback loops into your reinvention system. Have at least one person in your life who is allowed to reflect back what they see—both your growth and your gaps.

This isn't about criticism. It's about *clarity*. Identity is slippery. Sometimes we drift without realizing it. A trusted mirror keeps us honest.

And finally, use identity journaling as a regular practice. Weekly, ask yourself:

How did I live as Identity 2.0 this week?

Where did I revert to old patterns—and what triggered that?

What's next for this version of me?

This ongoing dialogue keeps your transformation alive. It makes growth a habit. Not a dramatic leap, but a continuous unfolding.

You stop waiting for breakdowns to force evolution. You begin choosing it—before life demands it.

Because the truth is, you are not just building a new identity. You are learning how to *live as a builder*. Someone who adapts, refines, and realigns by design. Not once. Not twice. But every time life asks: *Are you still the one steering the ship?*

In the final step, you'll bring it all together—creating a tangible, living document that becomes your *Identity Operating Manual*... and your companion for the life that's still unfolding.

STEP TEN

Build Your Identity Operating Manual

You've designed a new identity. Now you need a system to live by it, grow with it, and return to it when the world tries to make you forget who you are.

Most people don't forget who they are because they're weak. They forget because they don't have a system to remember. In the chaos of daily life, your higher self can get buried under deadlines, emotions, social roles, and survival patterns. That's why the final step in engineering your Identity 2.0 isn't philosophical—it's practical. It's about creating something tangible, accessible, and repeatable: a tool that anchors you to the identity you've chosen and helps you return to it over and over again. This is your Identity Operating Manual.

This manual isn't for show. It's not a vision board or a feel-good affirmation sheet. It's a personalized, evolving guide to *how you live, lead, decide, and adapt*. It should feel alive—something you revisit in moments of clarity *and* in moments of crisis. A lighthouse when you're lost. A compass when you're drifting. A power source when you're running low.

Here's what it includes:

Your Identity 2.0 Declaration

This is your foundational statement. Who you've decided to be. Not just traits, but truths. Not just goals, but *your way of being*. It should include:

A short summary of your chosen identity (e.g., "I am a grounded, powerful, creative leader who lives from purpose and speaks with clarity.")

The values that define how you move through the world

A few "I am" statements that feel emotionally real, not just aspirational

Your Purpose Alignment Map

Why you're doing any of this. What your life is ultimately in service of. Break this into two levels:

Your personal purpose: the internal force that gives your life meaning

Your contribution purpose: the external way you serve, lead, or create impact

Your Belief Reframe List

A side-by-side table:

On one side, the old beliefs that ruled you ("I'm not ready," "I need permission," "If I slow down, I'll fall behind")

On the other, the new beliefs you are reinforcing ("I'm ready now," "I create my own permission," "My power expands when I rest")

This isn't about denial—it's about conscious replacement.

Your Capability Plan

The learnable tools and skills and competencies that your new identity requires.

What do you need to learn, practice, or improve to sustain Identity 2.0?

What's your path for developing those capabilities (books, mentors, classes, reps)?

Your Behavior-to-Belief Bridge

Identify 3–5 keystone behaviors that reinforce your chosen beliefs.

"When I do X, I prove I am Y."
Example: "When I decline an unnecessary meeting, I prove I value my time."

Example: "When I speak my idea without overexplaining, I prove I trust my voice."

Your Ritual and Repetition Strategy

This is how you make your identity *sticky*.

Daily identity rituals

Weekly check-ins

Seasonal review prompts

Symbolic practices that remind you of who you are

Your Relationship Alignment Plan

A brief overview of:

Who reflects your new identity

Who may need boundaries or space

How you'll update the conversations, expectations, or dynamics that matter most

Your Environmental Anchors

The key changes you've made to your space, wardrobe, tools, and digital world

Your new "zones" of alignment (creativity, calm, health, leadership)

Any identity triggers you've placed in your daily path

Your Identity Drift Protocol

Because it *will* happen. You'll get overwhelmed. You'll regress. The old self will whisper. So this section is your pre-written plan:

"When I forget who I am, I will..." (revisit my statement, call my mentor, reread my journal, go to my environment cue, etc.)

"When I feel like I'm failing, I will remember..." (my purpose, my past progress, the cost of staying stuck)

"My recovery ritual is..." (walk, music, breathwork, silence, anything that resets your nervous system)

Your Next Evolution Sketch

Leave a section blank—or labeled "In Progress." This is for your future self. Write in pencil. This is where you begin to sketch the version after this one. The one that's still emerging. Because you are not done. You are not fixed. You are a living system. This is not the end. It's the foundation for everything that comes next.

Your Identity Operating Manual is your anchor. Your mirror. Your manifesto. Keep it printed, sacred, and accessible. Return to it when life gets loud. Revise it when life evolves. This is how you don't just transform once—but live as someone who evolves by design, not by accident.

And if you've made it this far, you've already done something most people never do: you've chosen to take responsibility for who you are becoming. You've stopped outsourcing your identity to your past. You've stopped pretending change is a mystery. And you've started to live as the creator of your life—not the product of your history.

This is the real power of Identity 2.0. It's not just that you've changed.

It's that you now know how to *change on purpose*.

Welcome to the life your old self didn't know was possible.

FINAL THOUGHTS

From the Author

Becoming the Architect of your Life

This Isn't the End — It's the Beginning

You didn't just read a book. You crossed a threshold. Page by page, question by question, you've walked yourself to the edge of something profound — the realization that your life is not a fixed script, but a living blueprint. Most people go their entire lives reacting to circumstances, clinging to old roles, mistaking busyness for purpose. But not you. You stopped. You paid attention. You took a flashlight into the basement of your identity and asked the hardest question anyone can ask themselves: *Who am I really — and who do I want to become?* That takes courage. Not the loud, performative kind. The quiet, relentless kind. The kind that chooses honesty over comfort. That kind that says, "I'm ready to see what's really been driving me." If no one's said it yet, let me be the first: I'm proud of you. Not because you've figured everything out — you haven't, and you don't need to. I'm proud because you've done something most people won't. You chose awareness. You chose responsibility. You chose to step out of the trance of who you've been told you are, and to begin the work of becoming who you were always meant to be.

What you've done here is not small. This book was not a passive experience. It asked you to go deep — to remember where your story started and to decide, with full authority, where it goes next. It invited you to leave behind identities that no longer serve you, beliefs that no longer define you, and behaviors that no longer reflect your values. That's not easy work. It's soul work. And now that you've started, there's no going back to sleep. You've tasted the power of alignment. You've glimpsed the possibility of living as your most authentic self. And even if you're not sure how it will all unfold, you've taken the most important step — you've remembered that you have the power to choose. To design. To build.

So no — this isn't the end. It's not even a conclusion. It's ignition. You didn't finish this book. You just started writing the most important chapter of your life. The one where you stop trying to fit into your past and start rising into your future. The one where you no longer wait for permission or validation. The one where you become the architect of your identity — and by extension, the architect of your life. Not by force. Not by pretending. But by choosing. Over and over again, until the life you're living reflects the truth you've reclaimed: you are not who you used to be. You are who you decide to become — starting now.

You Will Forget — and That's Okay

There will be days when all of this feels far away. You'll wake up tired, pulled back into old habits, and wonder if anything really changed. You'll second-guess yourself. You'll hear the voice of your former self — the one who plays it safe, keeps the peace, stays small — whispering that maybe this version of you was just a phase. That maybe this clarity, this courage, was just another passing high. That voice isn't a failure. It's a sign that you're in transition. Growth doesn't erase the past — it integrates it. And identity is not a light switch. It's a frequency. Some days, you'll be tuned in. Other days, static. And that's okay. Forgetting is part of the remembering. Regression is part of the rise. Just like a muscle being rebuilt, your new identity will sometimes feel shaky, even painful. That's not weakness. That's wiring.

So when you forget, when you slip back into old patterns, don't panic. Don't shame yourself. Just notice. Breathe. Return. That's what it means to live as Identity 2.0 — not to be perfect, but to be aware. To catch yourself drifting and choose again. That's why the Identity Drift Protocol exists — not as a one-time exercise, but as a lifelong compass. A quiet check-in when you feel overwhelmed. A grounding reminder when you feel off course. It's your tool for re-centering when life gets noisy, when your nervous system gets hijacked, when you find yourself reacting like the person you used to be. Because you will. We all do. But the difference now is this: *you'll notice sooner, and return faster*. Your old identity will whisper. But now, you have the volume knob. You've learned how to turn down the noise and turn up the truth. You've built awareness. You've built language. You've built a path back to yourself. And that is what makes you unstoppable — not that you'll never forget, but that you'll always remember your way home.

The World Will Try to Mirror Back the Old You

As you grow into your new identity, you may be surprised by how many people treat you exactly the same. You'll start speaking differently, choosing differently, showing up more fully — and yet, some people will still interact with you as if nothing has changed. Not because they're malicious. Not because they don't love you. But because the version of you they've memorized is easier for them to relate to.

People are comfortable with who you've been. They've learned how to predict you, count on you, categorize you. And when you begin to shift — even in subtle, life-affirming ways — it disrupts that pattern. Your clarity becomes their confusion. Your confidence becomes their confrontation. You'll hear it in the jokes they make, the doubts they raise, the subtle ways they try to remind you of "who you really are." That's not proof you're on the wrong path. It's confirmation that you're walking a new one.

You don't need everyone to believe in the new you. You need to believe in them first. You need to walk with your head high in the direction of your truth long before anyone else recognizes it. That's the work. And it can feel lonely at first. Which is why you must be intentional about who you let close. When you are rewriting your identity, the people around you become part of your ecosystem — reinforcing or resisting the change. That doesn't mean you need to cut people off. But it does mean you need to become discerning. Seek out spaces where your growth is normalized, not resented. Spend time with people who don't just accept the next version of you — they *expect* it. Create conversations that reflect who you're becoming, not who you've been trying to outgrow. Find or form communities where expansion is the baseline and self-reinvention isn't weird — it's welcome.

The truth is, external reinforcement always lags behind internal change. Your identity will shift long before the world updates its reflection of you. But if you wait for that reflection to give you permission, you'll stay stuck in the mirror of your past. Instead, keep moving forward. Speak the new language. Make the new decisions. Live in alignment with the version of you that no longer needs to be proven — only practiced. Because the moment you stop looking for others to confirm your change... is the moment it truly becomes yours.

Your Identity Is a Gift to the World

This journey was never just about you. Yes, you came here to reclaim your truth, to break out of old patterns, to rise into the next version of yourself. But what you may not have fully realized until now is that your transformation doesn't end with you — it *echoes*. Every time you make a choice that aligns with your Identity 2.0, you send a signal into the world: *It's safe to grow*. Every time you speak with clarity instead of performing for approval, someone else feels less alone. Every time you honor your boundaries, someone watching remembers they can too. You don't need a stage or a title to lead. You lead every time you show up as who you truly are — without apology, without armor, without shrinking to fit what others expect. That's what changes the world. Not perfection. Not performance. *Presence*. The willingness to live your truth out loud, even when your voice shakes. Even when your hands tremble. Even when no one claps.

The most inspiring people aren't those who have it all figured out. They're the ones becoming themselves out loud. The ones who fall, then rise with more grace. The ones who shift and stretch and question, not because they're broken, but because they refuse to settle. That's who you are now. Not someone who arrives — but someone who evolves. And your evolution invites others into their own. Whether you realize it or not, you're giving permission. To your friends. To your kids. To your clients. To your team. To the person next to you in the grocery store who senses something different in the way you carry yourself. Identity is contagious — not just the false ones we inherit, but the real ones we embody. And when you live from that place — when your actions, values, and vision are no longer in conflict — you become a mirror, not of who others think they *should* be, but of what it looks like to be *free*.

So let your life become an example — not of perfection, but of possibility. Walk into rooms without needing to perform. Speak without needing to impress. Move without needing to prove. Let your presence say what your words never could: *This is who I am now. And you're allowed to become, too*. That is the greatest gift you can give. Not your image. Not your accomplishments. But your alignment. The quiet power of someone who knows who they are — and chooses to live like it. Every day. Every breath. Every step forward from here.

Write the Next Version — On Purpose

Now you know the truth most people never discover: identity isn't static — it's strategic. It's not something you find, it's something you *build*. And you now have the blueprint. You've walked the levels. You've questioned the defaults. You've rewritten the inner code. You've stepped into alignment with the version of you that reflects your values, your desires, your truth. But the power of this work isn't in doing it once. It's in knowing you can return to it — again and again — every time life asks more of you. Because it will. New seasons will arrive. New roles, new goals, new chapters. And with them will come the invitation to evolve again. What once felt like your breakthrough identity will one day start to feel like your comfort zone. That's not failure — that's the signal. The sign that it's time to grow again.

You are not locked into this version of yourself. You are not meant to cling to Identity 2.0 as if it's your final form. Instead, let it be your foundation — the first true choice you've made about who you are and how you live. And when the moment comes — when you feel that familiar edge of discomfort or desire, that tug that says *there's more* — return to the process. Revisit the levels. Re-examine your beliefs, your values, your environment, your vision. Ask better questions. Give better answers. *Write Identity 3.0*. Then 4.0. Then more. Not because you're chasing something, but because you're choosing with clarity. Because your life is not a performance — it's a design. And you, now, are the one holding the pen.

Every time life evolves, you'll be ready.
Not because you're perfect.

Because you're practiced.

And that's what makes you powerful — not that you'll never be uncertain again, but that you'll never again be unconscious. You've learned how to build yourself on purpose. You've learned how to return when you drift. You've learned how to lead from alignment, not approval. And now, you get to live forward — not from the memory of who you've been, but from the truth of who you're becoming.

So write the next version. Let it be bold. Let it be different. Let it be yours.

You are the author now.
And the next chapter is already waiting.

A Personal Note from the Author

If you've made it here — all the way to the final words of this book — I want you to know something simple and real: *I see you*. Not just the version of you that shows up in public. Not just the one who gets things done, holds it all together, and rarely lets the mask slip. I see the you underneath that. The one who has always sensed there was more. The one who knows what it's like to quietly question your life, even when everything looks "fine" on the outside. The one who has lived through contradictions — showing up strong for others while feeling uncertain inside, achieving success while doubting your worth, staying loyal to versions of yourself that you've long since outgrown. I see you because I *am* you. This book wasn't written from a mountaintop. It was written from the middle of the very same work — the same reckoning, the same rebuild.

There was a time in my life when I looked successful on the surface and felt completely disconnected underneath. I had the titles, the respect, the certainty of other people's approval — and yet I would lie awake at night thinking, *What if I built a life around the wrong version of me?* I didn't have the language for it at the time, but I was grieving an identity I no longer fit into. And I was terrified of what might happen if I stopped playing the role I was known for. Who would I be without it? Who would I disappoint? What if I tried to step into something new and failed — publicly, spectacularly, painfully?

But slowly — through reflection, through pain, through mentors, through relentless curiosity — I began to see that identity wasn't something I had to wait for or stumble into. It was something I could build. On purpose. With clarity. With truth. With intention. Not to impress anyone. Not to escape who I had been. But to *align* with the person I was becoming — the one who had always been there beneath the noise. The moment I understood that, I got to work. And what you've just read is the result — not a perfect path, but a tested one. A framework I've lived. A process I return to every time I feel myself drifting from the version of me that's most true.

So if you're still wondering whether you have what it takes to live the next version of your life — let me say this plainly: *you do*. You already have. Every page you turned, every question you paused to consider, every moment you felt that lump in your throat and kept reading anyway — that was you stepping into your next self. You don't have to become anyone else. You simply have to become *fully* yourself. And if that sounds bold, or scary, or unfamiliar, good. That's how you know you're doing it right.

You're not broken. You never were. You're not behind. You're not too late. You're not too much or too little. You are exactly where you need to be — right here, at the threshold of your next chapter, with full authority to choose how it begins.

And if no one has told you yet today:
I believe in the person you're becoming.

More than that — I'm *grateful* for them. Because we need more people in this world who are willing to live honestly. Who are willing to lead quietly, consistently, through integrity and presence. Who are willing to grow — not for applause, but for alignment. If you choose to live that way — as Identity 2.0 and beyond — you won't just change your life. You'll help change the lives around you, whether you ever realize it or not.

So thank you. Thank you for reading. Thank you for staying. Thank you for daring to look inward. I wrote this book for you — and I wrote it *with* you, because we're on the same path. And no matter how the next chapter unfolds, I want you to carry one unshakable truth with you:

You're not alone. You're not broken.

And your story — *your true story* — is just beginning.

With deep belief in who you are, and fierce hope for who you're becoming,

— Keith

For more IDENTITY 2.0 Resources

Visit www.TheIDShift.com

Bibliography & Curated Reading Guide – *Identity 2.0*

For readers who want to go deeper into the ideas, methods, and inspirations behind this book.

I. Foundations of Identity and Change

If you've ever wondered why change sometimes sticks and sometimes falls apart, these works lay the groundwork. They explain the layered structure of human experience and why shifts at one level ripple through the rest.

- Bateson, G. (1972). *Steps to an ecology of mind*. Chandler Publishing.
  Introduces systems thinking and multiple levels of learning — the philosophical roots of the layered identity model used in *Identity 2.0*.

- Bateson, G. (1979). *Mind and nature: A necessary unity*. Dutton.
  Explores the deep interconnection between thought, behavior, and environment.

- Dilts, R. (1990). *Changing belief systems with NLP*. Meta Publications.
  Practical tools for reshaping limiting beliefs — a cornerstone of identity change.

- Dilts, R. (1994). *Strategies of genius, volume I*. Meta Publications.
  Shows how extraordinary thinkers operate, revealing patterns you can model.

- Dilts, R., Hallbom, T., & Smith, S. (1990). *Beliefs: Pathways to health and well-being*. Meta Publications.
  Demonstrates how beliefs dictate perception and outcomes.

- James, W. (1890). *The principles of psychology*. Henry Holt and Company.
  Classic work exploring habit, will, and self-perception — the original seeds of identity science.

II. Neuro-Linguistic Programming and Strategic Coaching

These titles teach you how to rewire your mind and influence change — in yourself and others — at the deepest levels.

- Bandler, R., & Grinder, J. (1979). *Frogs into princes*. Real People Press.
  The book that introduced NLP to the world — rapid change through language and perception shifts.

- Jacobson, S. (2016). *NLP coaching: An evidence-based approach for coaches, leaders and individuals*. Crown House.
  Explores how NLP patterns elevate coaching conversations to achieve sustainable behavioral and identity-level transformation.

- Madanes, C. (1981). *Strategic family therapy*. Jossey-Bass.

Foundational text on influencing patterns in relationships and systems.

- Madanes, C. (1990). *Sex, love, and violence.* W. W. Norton & Company.
  Powerful case studies in breaking destructive cycles through strategic therapy.

- Madanes, C. (1993). *The secret meaning of money.* Jossey-Bass.
  Reveals the hidden identity patterns that drive financial behavior.

- Madanes, C. (2007). *Relationship breakthrough.* Crown Archetype.
  Shows how shifts in identity transform every relationship.

- Robbins, A. (1991). *Awaken the giant within.* Free Press.
  Action-focused strategies for lasting personal change.

- Robbins, A. (1992). *Unlimited power.* Free Press.
  NLP techniques for peak performance and transformation.

III. Positive Psychology and Purpose

These works reveal why meaning, well-being, and self-actualization are essential to building a new identity that lasts.

- Csikszentmihalyi, M. (1990). *Flow.* Harper & Row.

Teaches how alignment between skill and challenge creates joy and mastery.

- Dweck, C. S. (2006). *Mindset*. Random House.
  Explains how adopting a growth mindset destroys the "fixed self" myth.

- Frankl, V. E. (1984). *Man's search for meaning*. Washington Square Press.
  A timeless guide to finding purpose in any circumstance.

- Maslow, A. H. (1943). A theory of human motivation. *Psychological Review, 50*(4), 370–396.
  Introduces the hierarchy of needs — how we grow into higher versions of ourselves.

- Maslow, A. H. (1968). *Toward a psychology of being*. Van Nostrand Reinhold.
  Explores self-actualization in depth.

- Seligman, M. E. P. (2002). *Authentic happiness*. Free Press.
  Research-based tools for lasting well-being.

- Seligman, M. E. P. (2011). *Flourish*. Free Press.
  Presents the PERMA model for a thriving life.

IV. Creativity, Vulnerability, and Self-Expression

Breaking old identity scripts often means reclaiming parts of yourself you've hidden. These books help you reconnect with authenticity and creativity.

- Brown, B. (2010). *The gifts of imperfection*. Hazelden.
  A guide to living fully in alignment with your real self.

V. Coaching and Facilitation Tools

These resources teach the conversational tools and strategies for guiding deep change in others — or in yourself.

- Cockerell, L. (2019). *Time management magic: How to get more done every day and move from surviving to thriving*. Morgan James.
  Offers practical systems for prioritization and focus—vital for aligning daily actions with strategic goals.

- Miller, W. R., & Rollnick, S. (2013). *Motivational interviewing*. Guilford Press.
  Client-centered methods for inspiring change without resistance.